T0214940

The Signal
The History of Signal Processing and How We Communicate

The Signal
The History of Signal Processing
and How We Communicate

Ted G. Lewis

CRC Press
Taylor & Francis Group
Boca Raton London New York

CRC Press is an imprint of the
Taylor & Francis Group, an **informa** business

CRC Press
Taylor & Francis Group
6000 Broken Sound Parkway NW, Suite 300
Boca Raton, FL 33487-2742

© 2019 by Taylor & Francis Group, LLC
CRC Press is an imprint of Taylor & Francis Group, an Informa business

International Standard Book Number-13: 978-0-367-22563-6 (Hardback)
International Standard Book Number-13: 978-0-367-22561-2 (Paperback)

Library of Congress Cataloging-in-Publication Data

Names: Lewis, T. G. (Theodore Gyle), 1941- author.
Title: The signal : the history of signal processing and how we communicate / Ted G. Lewis.
Description: Boca Raton, Florida : CRC Press, [2019] | Includes bibliographical references and index.
Identifiers: LCCN 2019004501| ISBN 9780367225612 (pbk. : alk. paper) | ISBN 9780367225636 (hardback : alk. paper) | ISBN 9780429275654 (ebook)
Subjects: LCSH: Telecommunication--History. | Signal processing--History.
Classification: LCC TK5102.2 .L49 2019 | DDC 621.382/209--dc23
LC record available at https://lccn.loc.gov/2019004501

Visit the Taylor & Francis Web site at
http://www.taylorandfrancis.com

and the CRC Press Web site at
http://www.crcpress.com

The stories of science are far more magnificent, grand, involved, profound, thrilling, strange, terrifying, mysterious, and even emotional, compared to the stories told by literature. Only, these wonderful stories are locked in cold equations that most do not know how to read.

– Liu Cixin, *The Three-Body Problem*

Contents

Preface

I AM FORTUNATE TO HAVE been born and raised during the rise of the Information Age—from the early years of the electronic digital computer and Shannon's theory to the mid-years of explosive growth under Moore's law, to the post-Internet years of commercialization and commoditization of information, information services, and Third Wave economics. It has been an exhilarating ride. It has also left some of us in the dust.

I fully subscribe to Liu Cixin's claim that science and technology are more exciting real-world topics than fiction, but it is often shrouded in complicated mathematics and professional jargon that is nearly impossible to penetrate without an advanced education in STEM (Science, Technology, Engineering, Math). Even specialists like myself often get lost in the details or left behind by rapid change. This is understandable: the barrier to entry into the understanding of the ideas of the scientists and technologists that built our modern world is high, and the price paid to keep pace is not always immediately rewarded. My first goal of this book is to identify the key ideas underlying modern communications technology, and to document the contributions of its inventors.

Recently, I began to notice the obituaries (online and elsewhere) of my idols piling up. The famous and not-so-famous STEM innovators I grew up with are disappearing. "The great ones are dying off," I told myself. As the cold reality sank in, I formulated a plan. I would dedicate my remaining few years to documenting the personalities and deeds of the Information Age pioneers. But, where should I start? I decided to start at the beginning—prehistoric times to the 1940s, through the remainder of the twentieth century, ending up when billions of people are about to accept the idea of pervasive, global communications without questioning, "How does this stuff work?" The stories I tell lead right to the start-over-again beginning of the new Internet age dominated by 5G. How we got here and how it all works is the subject of the following text. Each chapter begins with a story and, more or less, ends with technical details on how each milestone technology works. In fact, the technical details may be too much for some readers—in this case, I recommend you skip to the next section.

Of course many people responsible for such miracles as space travel and the Internet have been fully documented. The famous ones have been written about countless times. I noticed, however, a number of key personalities may be known throughout one or more technical communities, but are far less known among the intelligent lay population. Everyone knows who Steve Jobs is, but does everyone know who Irving Reed and Gustave Solomon are? Probably not. Steve Jobs may have brought us pervasive communication in the form of a smart phone, but reliable communication would not exist without Reed and Solomon. Who were they and what did they do? It is about time these pioneers are recognized.

My second motivation was more subtle than documenting the immortals of communications technology. Computers are the foundation of the Information Age, but communication technology is the foundation of the foundation! Without the phenomenal theories and practical applications of theory brought to us by the pioneers of communication, the Computer Age would perhaps have remained in the back office, hidden away as infrastructure like electricity or running water—critical to modern life, but not as transforming as the combination of communications and computing. The Information Age exploded when machines were endowed with the ability to talk among themselves. This is as revolutionary as the modern computer.

I chose *The Signal* as the title of this work because it is the signal that connects everything to everything else. I mean *signal* as in communication and also in the metaphorical sense as the link between and among people. How we communicate has been drastically modified by the signal in all of its human-made forms. Husbands and wives that once spoke to each other face-to-face, now substitute e-mail for much of their interaction. Over half of the human race is connected to one another by online platforms like Twitter and Facebook. Spacecraft report back to diminutive humans from 13 billion miles away. The meaning of the word "news" is an oxymoron because information traveling at the speed of light is instantly considered old by Internet standards. These subtle and not-so-subtle forms of communication are made possible by the signal and its perfection.

Perfect is the key word, here. What does perfection mean to the signal? Try the familiar parlor room game where people sitting in a circle whisper a simple message into the ear of the person sitting to their right. The silent whisper passes from person to person until returning to the initiator. What was the original message, and what returns from the circle of whisperers? In most cases, the original message is garbled and distorted, sometimes with humorous results. Without additional sophistication beyond the human whisper, the signal is easily scrambled. The signal is subject to distortion called *noise*. Much of this book is about noise and how to overcome it.

For much of the second-half of the twentieth century, pioneers of the Information Age waged a battle against noise. It became a technological struggle to balance clarity, power consumption, and cost against the intrusion of static, random distortions, and fading signals. According to the father of information theory, Claude Shannon, noise subtracts from information. Too much noise reduces information content to zero. Noise is devoid of meaning to humans. The battle against noise took decades to win. Only recently, within my adult life, have humans been able to defeat noise. And it was defeated in elegant and beautiful ways.

When I was born, analog signals were the dominant form of signaling. By the time I began my career in the 1970s, analog was well on its way to extinction. Digital and the so-called digital convergence has replaced analog as the dominant form of communication. We associate digital signals with the Internet, but it goes much further. Everything is digital—radio, television, music, movies, heart pacemakers, etc. Overthrowing analog was not planned. It simply happened, because digital is better. For one thing, digital means a machine can be programmed. Thus, digital signals facilitated the invention and rise of software. Whether a signal is transmitted or simply stored as a stationary message, the fact that it is digital means it can be processed by software. We still do not fully comprehend the profound significance of software. The software industry is still in its early stages of development.

As Liu Cixin says in the quote, "these wonderful stories are locked in cold equations that most do not know how to read." My mission, in addition to bringing your attention to the many unsung pioneers of the signal, is to decipher the cold equations that most people do not know how to read. This is not easy and will require the reader's dedication, because most of the amazing work done by the personalities I describe is extremely clever and deep. If the technology was easy to grasp, anyone could have invented it. For those readers less interested in the technical details, I have marked advanced sections as "Advanced" so the casual reader may skip them.

Finally, I want to acknowledge the help of John Gustafson, who corrected many of my errors and made important suggestions for improvement. However, as always, any errors or omissions are all mine.

Ted G. Lewis—February 2019

CHAPTER 1

The Blasphemy of Zero

IT WAS A PLEASANT spring day in the rolling hills outside of Brno, Czechoslovakia as Karel Absolon (1877–1960) hiked into the forest, crossed a rushing stream, and entered one of the many caves in the Moravian Karst system near the town of Blansko. He learned his trade at Charles University in Prague and in 1907 returned to Brno to become the custodian of the Moravian Museum, where he also became interested in the rich archeological treasures hidden in the Moravian basin south of Brno. His famous excavating began in 1924 and by 1926 he struck it rich when he discovered the ancient Venus of Dolní Věstonice—the oldest known ceramic statue in the world. A 25,000-year-old fingerprint of a child was found on the four-and-one-half-inch-tall figurine unearthed in 2004. But, the most interesting computing discovery made by Absolon was the *Gog computer*, as Charles Seife named it in 2000.*

I prefer to call it *Gog's memory stick*, because someone used it to store information using a simple code that worked for perhaps the next 25,000 years. Gog's memory stick has to rank as one of the longest lasting innovations in history. It is right up there with fire and language. Moreover, it suggests that intelligent—even ingenious people—have been around for a very long time. Information, its representation, storage, and communication are not new concepts.

---

* Seife, Charles (2000). *Zero: The Biography of a Dangerous Idea*. New York: Penguin Books. ISBN 9780140296471.

GOG'S MEMORY STICK

Gog's 25,000-year-old memory stick is a bone with notches scratched into it—perhaps used by cave dweller Gog to "count the deer [s]he killed, the paintings [s]he drew, or the days [s]he had gone without a bath," according to Seife.* Figure 1.1 illustrates Gog's memory stick with 55 notches, in groups of five and 25, suggesting that Gog counted by fives and 25s. Seife says the notched bone, "looks suspiciously as if Gog was counting by fives," perhaps because she had five fingers on each hand. She encoded the signal by copying her human hand.

After collecting about six or eight pelts, it became difficult for Gog to remember how many she had. So, Gog recorded her wealth by notching her memory stick each time she trapped a beaver. But, when her wealth exceeded about a dozen pelts, processing numbers becomes increasingly difficult unless the notches are conveniently grouped into *chunks*. Gog might have looked at her hand and equated it with five fingers and decided it made sense to do the same on the carved bone. Visually segmenting notches into groups of five each makes it easy for Gog to quickly recall her bounty. In a leap of intellectual insight, Gog grouped five hands together to form a unit representing 25 pelts, making it easier to record even larger numbers. Gog may have been the first human to code a signal by grouping information into chunks.

Gog did what humans are good at doing—making abstractions. Gog's brain was advanced enough to grasp the abstract concept of *psychological chunking*—big numbers are broken down into smaller numbers by grouping them together. When a literal handful of notches reached five, a chunk perhaps called a *hand* was substituted in place of the five notches. As numbers got even bigger, a chunk of five hands were grouped together once

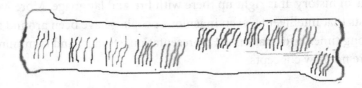

FIGURE 1.1 Gog's signal is a series of notches on a bone or counting stick. Each notch represented one unit of something Gog owned. The notches are grouped into chunks—five notches form a "hand," and five hands form another unit, perhaps called a Mammoth.

---

* Ibid., p. 6.

again, to form a grouping called a "herd," "flock," "bucket," or "bunch." Who knows what Gog actually called them, but chunks made it easier for Gog to process the data recorded on her memory sticks. The signal began to get more sophisticated as Gog's wealth grew. Chunking may have been the first information code designed to cut down on errors and track wealth.

Along with colleagues Noam Chomsky (1928–) and Jerome S. Bruner (1915–2016), George A. Miller (1920–2000) founded the field of cognitive psychology to study the many ways humans store and retrieve information. Unlike behavioral psychology, cognitive psychology lent itself to experimentation and measurement. Miller is known best for explaining how and why humans are such good chunking experts. By doing experiments in the early 1950s, Miller discovered that short-term memory capacity fell somewhere between five to nine items, or "seven, plus or minus two."* Chunk size depends on the type of information—around seven for digits, six for letters, and five for words.

When chunk size goes beyond the magical seven symbols, humans turn to abstractions that allow us to replace a chunk with a simpler signal. For example, gibberish, as illustrated by the following string of characters:

"THATTHATISISTHATTHATISNOTISNOT"

becomes meaningful when chunked:

"THAT THAT IS, IS, THAT THAT IS NOT, IS NOT"

Telephone numbers, social security numbers, and web page addresses are more easily recalled when formatted into chunks. Each chunk is limited to seven symbols, plus or minus two. If not, then grouping longer sequences of symbols into chunks of seven symbols reduces the cognitive load. Gog the cavewoman obviously had the cognitive ability to handle five symbols at once. She also had the ability to advance the chunking idea to code even larger numbers as groups of five.

---

* Miller, G.A. (1956). The Magical Number Seven, Plus or Minus Two: Some Limits on Our Capacity for Processing Information. *Psychological Review*, 63, pp. 81–97. Miller noted that humans can process information better if it is broken down into *psychological chunks* of approximately seven pieces, plus or minus two. This concept has become fundamental to how computer systems are designed and built, but even cavemen recognized the value of chunking 30,000 years ago.

Psychological chunking is one of the most primitive forms of encoding, and meaning extracted from chunks is one of the most primitive forms of decoding. The idea of using symbols to represent information, and chunking to encode/decode information is the basis of all of modern signal processing. Without these fundamental concepts, modern communication would not work.

Miller went on to become one of the earliest advocates of the "brain as computer" school of psychology. His career spanned the rise of the computer age, so it only seems natural that he adopted the modern electronic computer as a model of cognition. But, does the brain of a human work like a computer, or does a computer work like a human brain? The "brain as computer" model says humans possess memory just like computers do and we process information like computers. We even communicate information from person to person, just like computers. While the underlying technology is vastly different, rudimentary information-processing capability exists in both species. And yet, Miller's work leaves us wanting more. Exactly what is in a signal?

BIGGER SIGNALS

Gog must have been able to perform elementary arithmetic or rudimentary processing because she knew how to combine five hands to make a chunk representing 25 pelts. Perhaps Gog called this a Mammoth, because she could trade 25 pelts for one Mammoth—enough meat to last through the winter. Two chunks of 25 pelts each equals two Mammoths, and so on. This kind of simple arithmetic might have been difficult to do in a caveman's head, but simple to do by combining and separating notched bones. It is simply a coding problem.

Coding is the process of converting one set of symbols into another set of symbols such that meaning is preserved or even enhanced, information compressed, or errors reduced.

Gog added notched mammoth bones to her collection of bones to keep track of her mammoth meat supply. She knew she could trade five hands of pelts for a Mammoth. She might have broken off a group of five hands to "subtract" one Mammoth from the total and combined two bones to do "addition." Gog's memory sticks may even have traveled with her when she went shopping. In this way, Paleolithic humans communicated financial information to others across both space and time—a form of money transfer not unlike modern credit cards and physical money of today.

When her collection of bones diminished, she could go hunting once again, and when her cave overflowed with bones, she could sit back and enjoy life.

Gog's memory stick made it easier to encode and store information, process, and communicate information—the fundamentals of modern computing.

Great wealth and prosperity often come at a price. For one thing, expressing very large numbers in groups of fives on a bone soon requires very large bones and enormous patience for people that own lots of things, build big things, or travel long distances over long periods of time. Try notching the number 1,000,000 on a bone, or recording the number of laborers needed to build the pyramids on a pile of bones. Even worse, try adding and subtracting large numbers recorded on a pile of bones. Gog's memory stick soon became inadequate simply because its coding scheme lacked compactness.

About 20,000 years later, the Egyptians living on the Nile needed large numbers to record bountiful grain harvests and measure large structures like the pyramids. For example, to measure and record 123 cubits (about 64.4 meters), an ancient Egyptian accountant used a symbol called a *snare* to represent 100, a symbolic *heel* to represent 10, and a vertical line to represent single units. One hundred and twenty-three cubits was written as Θ∩∩III. Mathematically, $123 = 100 + 2(10) + 3$.

The idea of substituting symbols for chunks introduced by the Egyptians was so powerful the Greeks adopted a similar encoding: HΔΔIII. But, ancient Egyptians and Greeks still had a problem: how to encode even larger numbers like 1,000,000 and 10,000,000? Encoding 10 million requires eight different symbols—one for each position: ones, tens, hundreds, thousands, tens-of-thousands, hundreds-of-thousands, millions, and tens-of-millions. As ancient peoples got richer, they needed bigger numbers to account for their riches. The number system began to break down once again. The signal began to be buried in too much complexity.

The Babylonians, and other cultures at approximately the same time, began automating computation using an *abacus*. The abacus allowed anyone to perform simple addition and subtraction on large numbers by moving stones around, see Figure 1.2. The abacus introduced a new innovation in coding theory—a generalized stone symbol—that could be repurposed instead of creating a new symbol for every bigger and bigger chunk. Special symbols like the snare and heel were replaced with a positional notation like we have today. Unfortunately, the Babylonians started

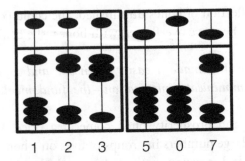

FIGURE 1.2 The decimal numbers 123 (left) and 507 (right), expressed by a base-5 abacus. The four lower stones represent units 0–4, and the upper stones represent chunks of 5. Lower stones are moved up to process units; and sliding an upper stone down means processing chunks of 5 units each. The number 7 is represented by one 5 and two 1's, e.g., (5 + 2).

out with base-60 symbols instead of base-10. Figure 1.2 illustrates how an abacus with stones representing chunks of size one and five generalized Gog's memory stick by making the stones movable and introducing the concept of a number's position. This new code used a symbol's position to encode more information.

The Babylonians needed one more thing—zero. Otherwise, how could 120 or 507 be represented? Without zero, a positional number system that repurposes the same symbols (stones) doesn't work. How would 120 be distinguished from 12, or 507 from 57? The abacus had no zero stone. Instead, it represented zero as "no stone." The Babylonians had no idea of how to carve "nothing" on a clay tablet. They simply left a blank space instead. The code got even tougher to decipher because zero was absent and the absence of something meant nothing to ancient accountants.

ZERO IS EVIL

Zero was a hard pill for Western society to swallow, because Pythagoras and Aristotle refused to acknowledge it. According to Seife, "the Greeks so despised zero that they refused to admit it into their writings, even though they saw how useful it was. The reason: zero was dangerous."* The great Pythagoras who gave the world the Pythagorean theorem for computing the length of the hypotenuse of a right triangle also gave the world a philosophy that hated zero. Pythagoras taught that harmonic forces govern the universe. These harmonic forces show up in the geometric shapes and

---

* Seife, p. 19.

numerical ratios needed to explain the natural world. He taught that it is *impossible* for a shape to have zero area or the ratio of nothing to something equals nothing (zero). Pythagoras could not conceive of dividing a number by zero or multiplying any number by zero to get another zero. For nearly two thousand years, Pythagoras's philosophy was the anchor that held back scientific progress in the Western world.

Pythagorean philosophy eventually gave way to the Aristotelian system, which dominated Western science and religion for far too long. Aristotle also banished zero, but for a different reason—to prove the existence of God. Aristotle's "proofs" almost always sidestepped the vacuum or void, as he called it, and zero was equated with the void. God's universe began in year one, not year zero. The Gregorian calendar introduced by Pope Gregory XIII in 1582 started in the first century with year one, rather than the zeroth century in year zero. This is why the twentieth century began in 1900—a century late.

The Greek influence, as wrong as it was, enjoyed an incredibly long reign. It was spread through the known world by Aristotle's student, Alexander the Great (356 BC–323 BC), and lasted until Elizabethan times, circa 1550. "Lurking underneath the veil of medieval philosophy, however, was a conflict. The Aristotelian system was Greek, but the Judeo-Christian story of creation was Semitic—and Semites didn't have such a fear of the void."* Eventually, this conflict would force pre-enlightenment era scholars to adjust their worldview, opening the floodgates to the scientific and industrial revolutions to follow. Suddenly, the signal got stronger because the symbol for nothing became something.

The break from Aristotle had to come from outside.

THE NOTHING AND EVERYTHING SIGNAL

Thanks to the Indians and Hindu philosophy, zero and infinity were saved and reintroduced into Western culture just in time to spur scientific and cultural revolutions like the *scientific revolution* (1543–1632) and the *age of enlightenment* (1620–1789). Not only did Indian mathematicians accept zero and infinity, they embraced them. Zero stood for nothing—the void—and infinity stood for everything—unbounded reality with no end. Both the Hindu god and twelfth-century Indian mathematician and astronomer Bhaskara (c. 1114–1185), had no quarrel with multiplying and

---

* Seife, p. 61.

dividing by zero.* He reasoned that any number divided by nothing produces everything, and any number multiplied by nothing produces nothing. The Hindu notation for nothing—a round goose egg—is still used today. The symbol for infinity, ∞, derived from the ancient endless "love knot," first appeared in Western mathematics in a book published in 1655 by John Wallis (1616–1703), one of Isaac Newton's most influential professors. The signal was coming back into focus.

The first Western civilization sighting of zero appeared in a book published in 876 CE.† It was a revelation and quantum leap forward in thought as well as information processing. Together with the positional number system that repurposed symbols, the full deck of ten digits became the bedrock of modern information coding. A fixed base such as ten (or two in the case of digital computers), positional power (ten or two raised to a power), negative numbers, and a standard representation of the most elementary units of information (ten or two numerals to represent basic elements of information) rounded out the system we have today.

Progress remained slow, however. Another 400 years passed while the Hindu system slowly diffused into Western society. Leonardo of Pisa (1180–1250), better known as Fibonacci (son of Bonaccio), is credited with spreading the controversial Hindu number system and Hindu mathematics throughout Europe. Fibonacci's father, a Pisan businessman living in North Africa, sent his son to Egypt, Syria, and Greece to study under Muslim scholars well versed in Hindu–Arabic mathematics. He mastered their system of coding and Arabic algebraic methods that far exceeded what was known in the West. After completing his education, Fibonacci returned to Europe and promoted the Hindu–Arabic system through a bestseller titled *Liber Abaci*, which was published first in 1202 and again in 1228. [A major accomplishment considering the printing press was not invented until circa 1440.]

ZERO REMAINS EVIL

The problem of zero (and infinity) that plagued the Greeks, Hindus, and Europeans up to the current milieu continues to plague modern computing, today. The fastest and largest supercomputer is easily stopped in its

---

* Bhaskara gives the first rigorous description of the decimal system using ten digits including zero. http://encyclopedia2.thefreedictionary.com/Bhaskara
† Boyer, Carl B. (1968). *A History of Mathematics.* John Wiley & Sons, p. 213.

arithmetic tracks by zero and infinity. The following examples illustrate the persistent problem with zero.

James Gleick (1954) tells the story of Ariane 5, the European Space Agency's large booster designed to leapfrog its competitors in the race to exploit the commercial potential of space. According to Gleick, the root cause of the Ariane 5 crash in 1996 was lack of a suitable code for infinity. The Ariane 5 computer simply could not handle a certain large number. ["Infinity" is defined as any number bigger than the largest number a computer can store.]

> It took the European Space Agency 10 years and $7 billion to produce Ariane 5, a giant rocket capable of hurling a pair of three-ton satellites into orbit with each launch and intended to give Europe overwhelming supremacy in the commercial space business. All it took to explode that rocket less than a minute into its maiden voyage last June, scattering fiery rubble across the mangrove swamps of French Guiana, was a small computer program trying to stuff a 64-bit number into a 16-bit space. One bug, one crash.
>
> Of all the careless lines of code recorded in the annals of computer science, this one may stand as the most devastatingly efficient. From interviews with rocketry experts and an analysis prepared for the space agency, a clear path from an arithmetic error to total destruction emerges. At 39 seconds after launch, as the rocket reached an altitude of two and a half miles, a self-destruct mechanism finished off Ariane 5, along with its payload of four expensive and uninsured scientific satellites. Self-destruction was triggered automatically because aerodynamic forces were ripping the boosters from the rocket.
>
> This disintegration had begun an instant before, when the spacecraft swerved off course under the pressure of the three powerful nozzles in its boosters and main engine. The rocket was making an abrupt course correction that was not needed, compensating for a wrong turn that had not taken place. Steering was controlled by the onboard computer, which mistakenly thought the rocket needed a course change because of numbers coming from the inertial guidance system. That device uses gyroscopes and accelerometers to track motion. The numbers looked like flight data—bizarre and impossible flight data—but were actually a diagnostic error message. The guidance system had in fact shut down.

This shutdown occurred 36.7 seconds after launch, when the guidance system's own computer tried to convert one piece of data—the sideways velocity of the rocket—from a 64-bit format to a 16-bit format. The number was too big, and an *overflow error* resulted. When the guidance system shut down, it passed control to an identical, redundant unit, which was there to provide backup in case of just such a failure. But the second unit had failed in the identical manner a few milliseconds before. And why not? It was running the same software.*

The Ariane 5 disaster happened for a very simple reason—the mathematically correct calculation became an approximation when translated into code and internal data. Technically, the control system was flawless, but when converted to a low-precision approximation, the math no longer worked. The code for signaling broke down. Luckily, nobody was killed.

The USS Yorktown (1983–2004) was one of the most sophisticated warships ever conceived and built by humankind when it was launched in 1983. The crew won the Atlantic Fleet's Top Gun award for outstanding performance in 1987. It won the Old Crow's award in 1991 for excellence in electronic warfare. Its list of accomplishments goes on for pages.† The ship was especially impressive because of its advanced computing power and highly potent missiles. Computers replaced sailors in every job possible, but the designers forgot one thing—the evils of zero.

The powerful and sophisticated Yorktown was stopped dead in the sea on September 21, 1997 by a "division by zero" error. The computer crash brought down all computers aboard and the entire network including the ship's propulsion system. A crewman accidentally entered a blank field into a database. The blank was treated as a zero, causing a divide-by-zero error, and crashing Microsoft Windows NT 4.0. The Yorktown was stalled for almost 3 hours, unable to steer, and unable to use its engines or weapons, until Microsoft Windows was restarted. Perhaps the Greeks were right: zero is a dangerous idea.

One of the reasons for system failures like those just described is that the real world operates in analog, while digital computers operate in digital. Analog signals assume continuous real-valued numbers with no gaps between successive values. Analog is closer to mathematics than digital.

---

* Gleick, James (1996). *A Bug and a Crash.* https://around.com/ariane.html
† https://en.wikipedia.org/wiki/USS_Yorktown_(CG-48)

Digital, on the other hand, assumes gaps—finite discrete-valued signals can only approximate real values. A digital machine like a digital radio, digital TV, or digital watch approximates real values by sampling them at intervals, leaving gaps in between. As a result, digital calculations may contain misleading errors.

The best we can do is use high-resolution (high-precision) digital numbers to represent the actual behavior of its analog equivalent. But, sometimes representing real numbers with high-resolution approximations fails. Consider the problem of locating the minimum value of a function y calculated and plotted in Microsoft Excel.

Figure 1.3 shows the same function y(x) calculated in Microsoft Excel over the interval $1.32 \leq x \leq 1.34$, but at three different resolutions:

$$\Delta x = 0.11$$

$$\Delta x = 0.011$$

$$\Delta x = 0.00015$$

That is, the Excel function is calculated at $x + \Delta x$, $x + 2\Delta x$, $x + 3\Delta x$,... for the three values of Δx. The differences are dramatic.

Figure 1.3a obscures the true minimum value entirely. It places the minimum at 1.32, which is far from the correct answer. Figure 1.3b begins to suggest something may be wrong, and Figure 1.3c is even more dramatic. The truth comes out as resolution increases by making intervals smaller and smaller. There must be a minimum near 1.33, but we cannot be sure. The signal is obfuscated by inadequate precision. Inadequate precision is a coding problem.

Unfortunately, none of the minimum values computed by Excel are correct. The true minimum value occurs at $x = 4/3$, and $y = -\infty$. In fact, Excel cannot compute the minimum value because it cannot process 4/3 exactly. All modern computers have this problem. Most use the *IEEE 754 Floating Point Standard* to encode approximations of the real numbers. It defines $-\infty$ as *Infinity*, and numbers it cannot represent as *NaN*—an abbreviation for "Not a Number." Furthermore, the IEEE 754 standard does not even attempt to define operations on *Infinity* and *NaN*. Instead, computers that use the IEEE 754 standard simply stop calculating when *Infinity* and *NaN* are encountered. The flaw is not restricted to Excel—it is a limitation shared by all information-processing machines that encode information with the IEEE 754 standard. This is a problem of representation

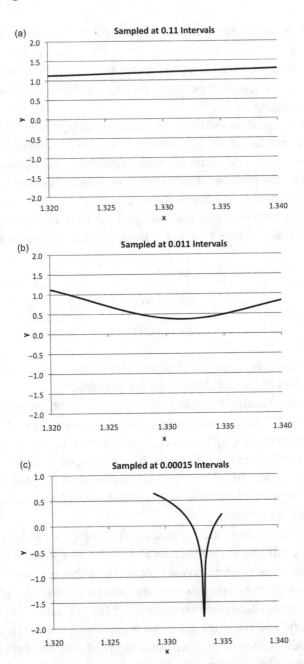

FIGURE 1.3 Microsoft Excel calculation of y(x) for three sampling intervals. The correct minimum value of y(x) is minus infinity, but depending on the sampling interval, Excel calculates incorrect minimum values ranging from −1.778 to 1.125. (a). Function y(x) sampled at intervals of $\Delta x = 0.11$; (b). Function y(x) sampled at intervals of $\Delta x = 0.011$; (c). Function y(x) sampled at intervals of $\Delta x = 0.00015$.

of information, which can have disastrous implications if not carefully considered.

Finite computation: Computations performed by a finite machine may contain inaccuracies, because a finite machine may only be able to approximate a real number. In some cases, the inaccuracy is so large that the results of computation are meaningless.

In the real world, all machines are finite so it is impossible to eliminate all computational errors. This has profound implications for modern computing machines just as it did for ancient mathematicians who struggled with the meaning of zero and infinity. The gap between precision and accuracy raises the question of whether we can trust the results produced by a machine. Note there is a difference between precision and accuracy.

Accuracy: A representation of a number is accurate if the difference between the value of the number and the value of its representation is zero:

$$\varepsilon = |\text{number} - \text{representation}| = 0$$

Otherwise the representation is inaccurate.

Precision: The precision of a representation is defined as the number of digits in the representation. Precision is a limitation of a finite representation, and therefore, may only approximate the exact value of a number.

A loss of precision in the onboard computer of the Patriot anti-missile missile caused it to miss its target, because rounding a number like $4/3 = 1.333\ldots$ to a less precise 1.33, and then multiplying it by a large number such as 10,000 yields a big error. Instead of $10,000 \times 4/3 = 13,333.33$, the rounded off calculation $10,000 \times 1.33 = 13,330$, which is off by 3.33. In the case of the Patriot missile, loss of precision led to loss of its intended functionality.

On February 25, 1991, during the Gulf War, an American Patriot Missile battery in Dharan, Saudi Arabia, failed to track and intercept an incoming Iraqi Scud missile. The Scud struck an American Army barracks, killing 28 soldiers and injuring around 100 other people. Patriot missile A report of the General Accounting office, GAO/IMTEC-92-26, entitled Patriot Missile Defense: Software Problem Led to System Failure at Dhahran, Saudi Arabia reported on the cause of the failure. It turns out that the cause was an inaccurate calculation of the time since boot due to computer arithmetic errors. Specifically, the time in tenths of second as measured by the system's internal clock was multiplied by 1/10 to produce the time in seconds. This calculation was performed using a 24 bit fixed-point register. In particular, the value 1/10, which has a non-terminating binary expansion, was chopped at 24 bits after the radix point. The small chopping error, when multiplied by the large number giving the time in tenths of a second, led to a significant error. Indeed, the Patriot battery had been up around 100 hours, and an easy calculation shows that the resulting time error due to the magnified chopping error was about 0.34 seconds.*

Loss of precision can have a snowball effect on loss of accuracy. A round-off error here can be magnified by an operation elsewhere in the calculation. The magnitude of the errors may become greater as the error propagates. The precision problem illustrated by the Patriot missile underscores the importance of coding the signal in a format that minimizes loss of precision. How information is encoded and represented matters.

A BETTER CODE (ADVANCED)

Proper coding of information can make possible the improbable act of communicating a weak signal 13 billion miles through space and time, as described in more detail in Chapter 3. Error correction matters, but precision and accuracy also matter. If the transmitted signal arrives without a flaw, it may still be useless unless it contains enough precision and accuracy to convey the true numerical meaning. The IEEE 754 code fails this test, because as shown earlier, its finite precision and failure to represent all possible real numbers introduces errors into the signal. Given that nearly every modern computer uses the IEEE 754 standard, we should be concerned, because most of us depend on modern digital computing to deliver safe and secure services.

A naïve programmer writing a program to compute the minimum value of the Excel function shown in Figure 1.3 faces a daunting task using IEEE 754 floating-point, because single and double precision floating-point numbers are still approximations. Using a Java language program, for example, and Δx intervals as before, a double precision calculation finds a minimum at 1.328999 for $\Delta x = 0.11$; 1.333348 for $\Delta x = 0.00015$; and never terminates for $\Delta x = 1.0 \times 10^{-8}$, because of loss of precision! Unless the programmer takes special care to test for IEEE 754 standard underflow

---

* https://ima.umn.edu/~arnold/disasters/patriot.html

through the **Double.MIN_EXPONENT** constant (−1022), Java software will miss the minimum value entirely, as did Microsoft Excel.

This bothered John Gustafson (1955), a computer scientist known for *Gustafson's Law*, reconstructing the first digital electronic computer (Atanasoff-Berry Computer—c. 1937–1942), and inventing the *Unum* number system—and later the *Posit* number system for more accurately representing floating-point numbers. According to Gustafson, floating-point signals go back a long way, and bring with them many headaches:

> A precursor of floating point arithmetic is embodied in the slide rule, invented by William Oughtread (1574–1660) in 1620. The slide rule multiplies and divides, but handles only mantissas. The user keeps track of the exponents. Computing machines with floating-point numbers (including exponents) were suggested by the Spanish inventor Leonardo Torres y Quevedo (1852–1936) in 1914; they were first implemented in Konrad Zuse's (1910–1995) computers, from the Z1 (1938) to Z4 (1945).*

Gustafson decided to do something about the mistreatment of infinity and low-precision calculations, so he invented a *universal number* system called *unum*.† Unum is a proposed alternative to the IEEE 754 standard.‡ Figure 1.4 illustrates how unum codes the signal, and how it differs from the IEEE 754 standard. The first difference is unum's variable-length fields for exponent and significand. Only the number of bits required to accurately represent a number are required. For example, the number 6.022×10^{23} requires only 8 bits to represent the exponent part and 12 bits to represent 6.022. Therefore, only 8 and 12 bits, respectively, are allocated. The e-size field and f-size field inform the hardware to use only $(7 + 1) = 8$ and $(11 + 1) = 12$ bits for these fields. The encoding of 6.022×10^{23} is shown in binary, hexadecimal, and decimal in Figure 1.4.

The exponential part is offset by 127 so both positive and negative exponents can be represented. Therefore, the exponent is $(205 − 127) = 78$. This is the power of two needed to scale up or down the fractional part.

$$2^{78} = 3.02231 \times 10^{23}$$

---

* Tichy, Walter (2016). The End of (Numeric) Error: An Interview with John L. Gustafson, Ubiquity, 2016(April). http://ubiquity.acm.org/article.cfm?id=2913029
† Gustafson, John L. (2015). *The End of Error: Unum Computing.* CRC Press.
‡ Tichy, pp. 1–14.

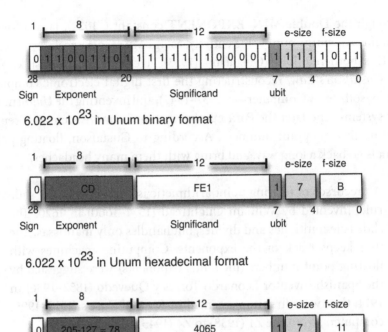

FIGURE 1.4 This unum format for encoding an approximation to the real Avogadro number in a finite computer uses 32 bits per word. Exponent and significand are variable-length, depending on the unum to be encoded. Here we assume they are 8 and 12 bits long, respectively, but they could be longer or shorter.

Next, the significand contains a hidden bit that is always 1, so the decimal value of the significand is actually $1 + 4065/2^{12} = 1.9924\ldots$ decimal. Therefore, the decoded unum is 3.02231×10^{23} times 1.9924:

$$1.9924(2^{78}) = 6.0217 \times 10^{23}$$

The sign bit is zero because the sign is positive. Unums use only the number of bits needed to maintain precision. Thus, the length of significand and exponent may vary. At the other extreme, the ubit signals when there are not enough bits to represent a number, exactly. But, how does unum deal with overflow, divide by zero, and infinity? The *ubit* field signifies the presence of these anomalies, indicating that an approximation has taken place and accuracy is compromised. When the ubit is set, and therefore the unum is an approximation, unum places the computation in a ubox by setting upper and lower bounds on the result. The bounds on an ubox are calculated by dropping a bit—the lower bound—and adding a bit—the upper bound. For example, a ubox for the number shown in Figure 1.4 is $(6.0209 \times 10^{23}, 6.0224 \times 10^{23})$ because the exact result lies between round-off (1 bit less) and round-up (1 bit more).

$$\left(1 + \frac{4064}{4096}\right)2^{78} < X < \left(1 + \frac{4066}{4096}\right)2^{78}$$

The number used in this example is *Avogadro's number*, which is 6.0221415×10^{23} in single precision. This number lies in the ubox, hence ubox encloses the exact real number, even though it cannot represent the exact number, exactly!

If unums were used by Microsoft Excel to find the minimum value of the function in Figure 1.3, it would have put the location of the minimum (minus infinity) in a ubox bounded by (1.33203125, 1.3359375) assuming a 19-bit significand. And, if Excel implemented the log(x) function in unums, it would place the minimum value of the function in Figure 1.3 in the interval $(-\infty, -4.84375)$. The exact minimum value, of course, is $-\infty$.

Like the ancient Hindu–Indian and Arabic mathematicians, unums are not afraid of zero and infinity. Table 1.1 summarizes 19-bit unum encodings of infinity.[*] Note that infinity is an exact number. This means it can participate in calculations without causing an error. Here is what Gustafson says about computing $x = (1/0)(0/1)$:

> With type 2 unums, 1/0 becomes $\pm\infty$, and (0/1) is simply 0, of course. The product of $\pm\infty$ and 0 is the entire extended real number line, $[-\infty, \infty]$. With type 1 unums, the result is NaN, which is not very informative. It's 'not a number' because it's a set of numbers. A central idea of unums (type 1 or type 2) is to embrace the possibility that the correct answer to a calculation can be a set of numbers and not just a single exact number.[†]

Unums are still limited by the finite precision of a finite computer but they can do computations that the IEEE 754 standard cannot do.

TABLE 1.1 Some Special Unum Numbers Using Gustafson's
Encoding, S|F|E|ubit|F_size|E-size, where S is the sign, the
significand F contains F-size = 8 bits, and the exponent
E contains E-size = 4 bits

Unum Name	Meaning	Value
posinfu	Positive infinity	0|11111111|1111|0|111|11
neginfu	Negative infinity	1|11111111|1111|0|111|11
qNaN	Quiet NaN	0|11111111|1111|1|111|11
sNaN	Signaling NaN	1|11111111|1111|1|111|11
maxrealu	Largest finite unum	0|11111111|1110|0|111|11

In addition, they bound the inexact calculation inside a ubox interval. Regardless of the coding scheme used, all approximations of the real numbers are just that—approximations. But unums tell you they are approximations, whereas the IEEE 754 standard does not.

Mapping the reals: All finite computing systems approximate the real number system, because there are a countably infinite number of rationals and an uncountably infinite number of irrationals. Only unums report the approximation.

COMMENT

The way information is encoded matters. An encoding like Gog's bone, the abacus, IEEE 754 floating-point, or Gustafson's unums can make the difference between successful versus failed rocket launches and the validity of an important spreadsheet answer.

The signal is only as good as the encoding and decoding algorithms used to send and receive information over noisy channels limited by precision and accuracy. The entire global communications infrastructure depends on information coding algorithms like IEEE 754, unums, and others (to be discussed). Everyone planning to travel by airplane or automobile, ride in an elevator to the top of a 100-story building, and communicate securely over the Internet should ask if they work properly, and if they can be trusted to yield the correct answers.

This is the rest of the story.

CHAPTER 2

Most People Think
I Am Dead

I INTRODUCED MY WIFE TO Richard Hamming at a garden party in the early 1990s. He was wearing a loud red-white-and-blue plaid blazer and was about to bite into a cheesy cracker as we walked up to say hello. I said, "Molly, this is Richard Hamming. Dick, this is my wife Molly." He said, "Do you know who I am?" My wife had taken a number of computer science courses in her undergraduate days, so she knew about the Hamming code. "Yes, you are the Hamming code guy." Hamming quipped, "Oh, most people think I am dead." And it was true. Most people, of course, don't know what Hamming the man or Hamming the code is, and the people that did know who Hamming is on that sunny day in Monterey, California, likely thought he was dead. Like many great figures in science, if you are a famous scientist, the general public likely thinks you are dead.

Richard Hamming (1915–1998) joined the Manhattan Project in 1945 where he programmed some of the earliest digital computers. He recalls a conversation with a Manhattan Project colleague: "Some of us are worried that the atomic bomb might not stop eating up the oxygen until it is all gone. What makes anyone think fission stops once it is started?" He explained that if the bomb builders at the Los Alamos Laboratory were wrong, it wouldn't matter, because no one would be around to blame him!

After leaving the Manhattan Project, Hamming went to work for AT&T Bell Labs where he rubbed elbows with Claude Shannon and John Tukey. Shannon and Tukey developed exotic theories of information and coding, while Hamming stumbled onto a more practical and personal problem—his computer program produced incorrect results after running for days because of hardware errors committed by the computer. He would start the lengthy program running on a Friday evening only to arrive on Monday morning to find a single bit had destroyed the entire weekend's calculations. Hamming set about solving this problem, and the solution became known as the Hamming code. It was the first error-correcting code for digital information processing, and set off years of self-correcting code research leading to elegant codes like the Reed–Solomon, CRC, Turbo, polar code, and others.

Hamming was one of the first pioneers to run into the problem of precision and accuracy of computations based on the weak infrastructure of digital computers. But his problem was compounded by the inadequacy of early computing machines plagued by random errors called *noise*. Inaccuracy due to round-off errors was further compounded by errors introduced by accident. How could a deterministic machine make random mistakes? Every signal contains bonafide information plus unwanted noise:

$$\text{Signal} = \text{Information} + \text{Noise}$$

Hamming's job was to separate the noise from the information. He not only succeeded, but he found a way to detect and then correct errors caused by noise in what became known as the Hamming code. The Hamming code was the first code to find and correct random errors in a signal represented by a string of bits.

Like so many great ideas, the Hamming code (1950) is rather simple. It says that the number of errors that can be detected is one greater than the minimum Hamming distance between any two code words:

$$\#\text{Detected} = (d-1); d: \text{the minimum Hamming distance}$$

Suppose we use the numbers 0, 1, 2, 3 as code words. They can be expanded into binary numbers 00, 01, 10, 11. The minimum Hamming distance is the minimum number of bits that differ. In this case, 00 differs from 01 and 10 by one bit, and 11 by two bits. Similarly, 01 differs from 00, 10, and 11 by one bit, etc. The minimum Hamming distance is one. This means $d=1$ in the aforementioned formula. Therefore:

$$\#\text{Detected} = (1-1) = 0.$$

If we assign the 2-bit numbers 00, 01, 10, 11 to a code, then no errors can be detected because there is not enough redundancy in the code. In order to detect an error, we must incorporate redundancy in the code such that the minimum Hamming distance is at least two. Hamming's idea was to add *salt* to the code, such that there is extra space between code words. Then his code would use these "holes" between valid numbers to find and correct errors, because the erroneous signals fall into these holes. For example, adding a third bit to the simple two-bit code increases the minimum Hamming distance: 000, 001, 010, 011; see Figure 2.1a. If an error occurs it will be exposed as a fraud because it will fall into a "forbidden hole," reasoned Hamming.

Hamming defined code words as valid plus redundant symbols taken together so that if a word falls into one of the holes created by adding more bits to the code, it must be an error. But there is a limit to how many errors can be detected and corrected using redundancy to expand code words. A Hamming code can correct E errors if the minimum Hamming distance (size of holes) between any two of its code words is at least 2E + 1, or:

$$\#\text{Corrected} = (d-1)/2.$$

More redundancy means more ability to detect and then correct an error. The "valid" code words are a subset of the expanded words. Therefore, words that fall into the space between legal code words must contain errors. Hamming had found a way to separate out the subset of valid words from the allowable words. The problem of his day was ensuring the correctness of signals stored on magnetic tapes and magnetic memory, where spurious magnetic surges introduced noise. Using his controlled redundancy solved the problem of the day.

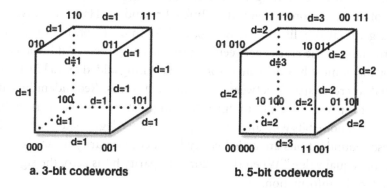

a. 3-bit codewords   b. 5-bit codewords

FIGURE 2.1 Hamming cubes for H(3, 3) and H(5, 3) shows how adding redundant bits increases the minimum Hamming distance from d = 1 to d = 2.

This was a huge breakthrough in the battle to separate information from noise in the signal. Not only had Hamming found a way to encode the signal to preserve its information, he had established a beachhead for further development in harsher environments where noise is bursty and sometimes drowns out the signal nearly entirely. It was the beginning of a long series of improvements that continues, today. And, most people thought he was dead long after everyone in computing used his method of securing information on a daily basis.

THE HOLES IN THE FIRST CODE

The size of the hole between code words in Hamming codes is the minimum Hamming distance. This distance determines how many errors can be detected and corrected. A simple way to calculate the minimum Hamming distance between a pair of binary numbers is to count the number of 1's resulting after you *exclusive OR* (XOR) them. The XOR operation is very simple. If two bits are the same, the result of XOR is zero; otherwise it is one. Therefore, the number of 1's in the result is equal to the number of bits that differ.

Here are some examples:

$$(110)\,XOR\,(101) = (011), \text{so } d = 2$$
$$(001)\,XOR\,(010) = (011), \text{so } d = 2$$
$$(010)\,XOR\,(000) = (010), \text{so } d = 1$$
$$(011)\,XOR\,(011) = (000), \text{so } d = 0$$

Intuitively, if two code words are far apart in terms of the Hamming distance, one will not overlap another one unless there is an error in at least one of the code words. That is if S = Info + Err, and the Hamming distance is large, then it is likely that Err = 0, and S = Info. If not, then the code word "falls in the cracks between" legitimate code words. And when this happens, it must be due to an error. So, Hamming added extra bits to the signal to create spaces between adjacent code words. Redundant bits are added to increase the minimum Hamming distance so that it is highly likely that noise bits will fall into the space between legitimate code words. These redundant bits are called *parity bits*, because parity means "equality," or "equal value." When the redundant parity bit is zero, the signal is equal to the information.

Errors in the signal can be detected and corrected by adding a sufficient number of redundant checking bits, called parity bits, to the code word.

Figure 2.1 Illustrates the idea of compensating for mistakes in the signal by adding redundant parity bits. Figure 2.1a shows that 3-bit code words are separated by 1 bit position, so d = 1. Therefore, d–1 = 0 errors can be detected. Figure 2.1b shows that adding two bits of redundancy to the 3-bit signal in Figure 2.1a separates code words by at least d = 2 positions. Thus, d–1 = 1 error can be detected. More generally, an H(n, k) code contains (n–k) redundant bits so d = (n–k) and (n–k–1) errors can be detected. For example, a popular Hamming code is H(7,4), so d = 7–4 = 3. This code can detect d–1 = 2 errors and correct (d–1)/2 = 1 error. Seven bits fit nicely inside most digital computers, so the H(7,4) code is used in many computer systems.

Hamming applied his code to single-bit errors. Multiple-bit error correction codes such as the Reed–Solomon code came years later. Nonetheless, the Hamming code found many uses because of its simplicity. Specifically, early tape storage devices were practically useless without the Hamming code. Even modern devices like pin-coded locks use Hamming codes to detect errors. When I get my car washed, the pin is encoded in a simple Hamming code such as 5483, which sums to an even number. If not, the pin must be a fraud.

The following is a complete example using even-parity error-checking bits. An even-parity bit is 0 if we count an even number of 1 bits in the signal, and 1, otherwise. By adding a handful of redundant even-parity bits to the signal, this code guarantees correctness. It can detect and remove an error if it exists.

EXAMPLE OF H(7, 4) CODE WORD (ADVANCED)

The H(7, 4) code is popular because it encodes 7-bit tape recorders, minicomputer words, and other early digital devices that roamed the landscape of the 1950s and 1960s. It is also simple enough to illustrate Hamming's brilliance. Consider a signal containing the binary information 1011. The H(7, 4) code leaves room for three even-parity checking bits to check on these four information bits. Even parity means the sum total of checking bit plus information bits must be an even number. In a binary computer, this is guaranteed when the number of 1s in a string of bits is even. Bits are identified by their positions, labeled from left-to-right as shown:

Location	1	2	3	4
Information	1	0	1	1

The first step is to open up "holes" at powers of two locations where we can insert the checking bits. The signal mentioned in the following paragraphs illustrates this with locations 1, 2, and 4, opened up for parity bits set to zero or one in order to enforce even parity. Hamming's clever idea was to place a checking bit in each of these positions to check on bits "in front of it," reading the code word from right to left, or backward from position 7 to position 1. Thus, p1 checks on bits 3, 5, and 7; p2 checks on bits 3, 6, and 7; and p3 checks on bits 5, 6, and 7. Note how checking bits cover more than one information bit. This redundancy is why the Hamming code works so well—by overlapping the covered information bits, Hamming added enough redundancy to locate an erroneous bit and correct it even if the checking bit is wrong.

	1	2	3	4	5	6	7
Code word	p1	p2	1	p3	0	1	1

Applying the rules for parity yields the following code word, which is sent across a noisy channel of some sort as a signal. The checking bits are underscored in the signal to distinguish them from information bits.

$$p1 = 1+0+1 = 2 \Rightarrow 0 \text{ because 2 is even}$$

$$p2 = 1+1+1 = 1 \Rightarrow 1 \text{ because 1 is odd}$$

$$p3 = 0+1+1 = 2 \Rightarrow 0 \text{ because 2 is even}$$

	1	2	3	4	5	6	7
Signal	0	1	1	0	0	1	1

Why embed checking bits at powers of two locations in the signal? This was perhaps a way to save hardware, which was very expensive in the 1940s and 1950s. Powers of two are achieved by simple shifts. A circuit can multiply a binary number by two by shifting left and divide by two by shifting right. The first checking bit is located at position 1; the second at $2 \times 1 = 2$; the third at $2 \times 2 = 4$; etc. Each position is computed from the previous one by a simple shift. The index register of the position counter needs to contain only three bits and a shifter to generate the position indices:

1: 0001

2: 0010

4: 0100

But I digress. What happens when an error occurs? For example, suppose the information 1011 is encoded, transmitted, and received at the other end as 1111. The signal arrives with the erroneous bit as follows:

	1	2	3	4	5	6	7
Signal	0	1	1	0	1	1	1

Repeating the even-parity calculations on the three checking bits quickly detects one or two errors:

$$p1 = 1+1+1 = 1 \Rightarrow 1 \text{ because 1 is odd. This should be 0.}$$

$$p2 = 1+1+1 = 1 \Rightarrow 1 \text{ because 1 is odd.}$$

$$p3 = 1+1+1 = 1 \Rightarrow 1 \text{ because 1 is odd. This should be 0.}$$

This Hamming code can detect d–1 errors and d = 7–4, so 2 errors can be detected but only (d–1)/2 = 2/2 = 1 error can be corrected. Assuming there is only one error in the example signal, we must locate it before it can be corrected. This means untangling the interlocking covers of p1, p2, and p3. The process of untangling the overlapping parity checks is called finding the *syndromes*. This is a strange term typically used in the medical profession. "A medical syndrome is a set of medical signs and symptoms that are correlated with each other and, often, with a particular disease or disorder. The word derives from the Greek σύνδρομον, meaning concurrence."* What is the concurrence between a parity check and an error?

Consider the pattern established by the coverage of the three parity-checking calculations just described. Checking bit p1 covers bit positions 1, 3, 5, and 7; p2 covers positions 2, 3, 6, and 7; and p3 covers positions 4, 5, 6, and 7. These covers overlap in a particular manner that allows us to triangulate an error by concurrence, i.e., matching the syndrome vectors against the signal treated as a vector. Note the overlapping pattern in the syndrome vectors as shown, where a 1 indicates a match between signal bit position and even-parity calculation:

Syndrome Vectors	1	2	3	4	5	6	7
p1	1	0	1	0	1	0	1
p2	0	1	1	0	0	1	1
p3	0	0	0	1	1	1	1

---

* https://www.google.com/search for syndrome

Matching or "concurring" is done by multiplying the signal and syndrome vector, summing the products, and remembering to replace even numbers with zero and odd numbers with 1. Here we go with the signal containing 0110111.

	1	2	3	4	5	6	7	Sum
Signal	0	1	1	0	1	1	1	
p1	1	0	1	0	1	0	1	
Multiply	0	0	1	0	1	0	1	3 => 1

	1	2	3	4	5	6	7	Sum
Signal	0	1	1	0	1	1	1	
p2	0	1	1	0	0	1	1	
Multiply	0	1	1	0	0	1	1	4 => 0

	1	2	3	4	5	6	7	Sum
Signal	0	1	1	0	1	1	1	
P3	0	0	0	1	1	1	1	
Multiply	0	0	0	0	1	1	1	3 => 1

The sums are actually binary digits that identify the location of the erroneous bit. That is, 101 is the binary equivalent of decimal 5, which is the offending bit position. Therefore, bit 5 in the received signal is an error. Flip it from 1 to 0 to correct it. The corrected signal is 0110011.

This Hamming code is 57% efficient because 3/7 of the bits are consumed in error detection and correction. Modern codes are much more efficient, but keep in mind Hamming was the pioneer who started the revolution. Others followed his path decades later, but he opened the floodgates of innovation by showing how redundancy is used to detect and correct errors in signals subject to noise. The Hamming distance provided a key to quantifying redundancy in terms of the "space between and among code words" that allowed for rigorously defining the number of errors that can be detected and corrected.

Here is a list of other Hamming codes that have been used over the past 70 years. Note how efficiency increases with size of code words.

Hamming Code	Detect	Correct	Efficiency
H(3, 1)	1	0	33%
H(7, 4)	2	1	57%
H(15, 11)	3	1	73%
H(31, 26)	4	2	84%
H(63, 57)	5	2	90%
H(127, 120)	6	3	94%

WHAT IS INFORMATION, ANYWAY?

By the twentieth century, technologists were getting close to understanding the true nature of numbers and computation. Numbers were useful for encoding and recording information; mathematics facilitated processing; and written documents like books communicated the information to anyone who could read. This capability emerged mainly through the development of Eastern mathematics and Western printing. But scientists and technologists of the early twentieth century still lacked a theory for what we call "information" until Claude Shannon (1916–2001), the *Father of Information Theory*, published his famous paper and book in 1948, and 1949, respectively.[*][†]

Shannon's work was revolutionary, but his theory of information was not the first or last time he made an indelible mark on the world's best thinkers. A decade earlier, Shannon wrote a Massachusetts Institute of Technology Masters degree thesis on circuit design that became the recipe for how to build digital computers from simple electronic circuits. He showed how electronic circuits designed to be equivalent to Boolean logic are used to construct digital computers. Most of today's computer and communication hardware technology rests on Shannon's work.

Shannon, a distant cousin of Thomas Edison (1847–1931), rubbed elbows with the most brilliant computer scientists of his time, even though the field of computer science had not been defined, yet. While at MIT, he worked on Vannevar Bush's (1890–1974) Differential Analyzer—an analog computer—and in 1943 he spent time with Alan Turing (1912–1954), known for the Turing Machine, Turing's Test, and breaking the Enigma

---

[*] Shannon, Claude E. (1948). A Mathematical Theory of Communication. *Bell System Technical Journal*, 27(3), pp. 379–423. doi:10.1002/j.1538-7305.1948.tb01338.x.

[†] Shannon, Claude E. and Warren Weaver (1949). *The Mathematical Theory of Communication*. University of Illinois Press. ISBN 0-252-72548-4.

code during WWII. In 1940, he met Albert Einstein (1879–1955) and Kurt Gödel (1906–1978), the famous logician, mathematician, and philosopher.

Later in life, Shannon co-invented the wearable computer with ex-student and colleague Edward O. Thorpe (1932–) in the early 1960s, and used his understanding of probability theory and information theory to earn a fortune playing the stock market.* He and Thorpe used a custom-built wearable computer to win games in Las Vegas. He was one of the earliest artificial intelligence researchers to use computers to play chess. Perhaps most important, he was an excellent juggler, unicycle rider, and renowned for building a robotic box with a lid and switch that, when toggled, caused the lid to open, a mechanical arm to pop up, turn the switch off, and return to the box.

Until Shannon published his information theory, few people knew what information was, how to measure it, or how information and codes for error correcting were related. It seemed that numbers were simply numbers and the symbols representing numbers were simply symbols. What about symbols that represent letters of the alphabet, or symbols that represent the color of a dot on a screen? To Shannon, all of these symbols were different forms of information, but information, nonetheless. Why differentiate alphabetic characters from numerical characters and images on a screen or printed page? After all, all forms of information are simply encoded messages. And to make these messages usable, they have to be translated into signals that communicate between earth and Voyager II, or between two people sitting in the same room.

Shannon separated the representation of information (encoding symbols) from its meaning. He further observed that representation in the form of symbols like "3.14159," "cat," and RED, is a code for something rather than the meaning of something, itself. Without an interpretation or meaning, the string of characters "dog" is simply *data*. To extract information from data, we need a person or machine to interpret it. Figure 2.2 illustrates this simple idea. Meaning is encoded into symbols (the signal) and perhaps stored or moved until it is retrieved and converted back into meaning. The encoded signal "d-o-g" has an interpretation that is separate

---

* Thorp, Edward O. (1962, 1966). *Beat the Dealer: A Winning Strategy for the Game of Twenty-One*. Random House. It presented the first scientific system ever devised for a major casino gambling game and revolutionized the game of blackjack—card counting.

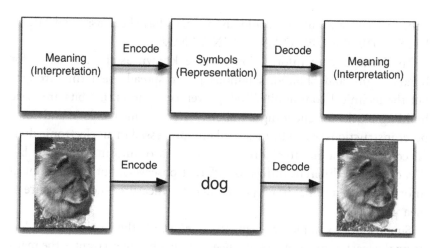

FIGURE 2.2 Signals encode information independent of its meaning. The English code for *dog* is different than the French (*chien*) and yet they communicate the same meaning. Do "dog" and "chien" communicate the same information? They do if the encode/decode process is unambiguous and lossless.

from how the meaning of dog is encoded. The English word "dog" is only one possible encoding. The same meaning or image of a dog might be encoded in Russian, French, or Chinese symbols. It is the efficiency of this encoding in a noisy environment or transmission channel that concerned Shannon, and not it's meaning. He reasoned that the information content of a signal can be measured without concern for its meaning, which he left up to linguists and psychologists.

By stripping away the efficiency of coding from meaning, Shannon was able to define information in terms of the number of bits used to encode a signal. Mathematically, the logarithm of the numerical code equals the number of bits in the code. We use $\log_2(x)$ to find the number of bits in x. Shannon went even further. He defined information in terms of the number of bits that are likely to occur in message x. Thus, his famous formula for information, $\log_2(p(x))$, tells us the number of bits likely to occur in a message x that occurs with probability p(x).

What was Shannon's reasoning for defining information in terms of the likelihood of symbol x appearing in a message? He reasoned that information can be broken down into elemental pieces through a very simple decision process—a series of *yes* versus *no, on* versus *off, up* versus *down,* or *one* versus *zero* decisions. These decisions are assigned a *binary digit* of either zero or one, but they could just as easily have been assigned TRUE/ FALSE, ON/OFF, UP/DOWN, or YIN/YANG.

The basic unit of information became known as the *bit*—short for binary digit—and Shannon's famous paper spread the term throughout the technical community. Today, everyone knows that bits are basic building blocks for encoding numbers, letters, sounds, colors, and computer instructions. Everything stored and processed in an electronic digital computer is a bit. Therefore, the basic unit of information is the bit. Bits can mean different things to different observers, but the amount of information in a signal is a type of efficiency measure—not a measure of meaning.

Suppose for example, we want to code/decode the English letter "m" using the least number of bits. We need enough bits to guarantee the mapping from "m" to a unique string of bits corresponds with only the letter "m" and nothing else. But we don't want to use too many bits, because that would be wasteful. A quick way to do this is to order the list of 26 characters in the English alphabet as shown in Figure 2.3, and then use Shannon's decision process to determine the number of bits of information needed to select "m" from the English alphabet with 26 letters.

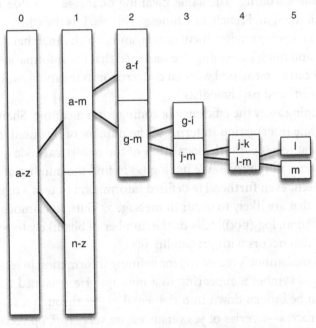

FIGURE 2.3 It takes five yes/no decisions to isolate the letter "m" from the 26 letters of the English alphabet using a divide-and-conquer decision tree as shown here.

Divide the list into (roughly) equal halves (13 letters, each) and ask, "Which half contains the letter 'm'?" It is in the first half, so the second half is discarded, and the search for "m" repeated on the remaining half. Once again, divide the list into (roughly) equal halves (7 and 6 letters, respectively) and ask, "Which half is the letter in?" This time it turns out that "m" is in the second half. Repeat this divide-and-conquer decision process until "m" is the only symbol remaining. How many decisions were made? The number of "yes" or "no" decisions equals the number of bits required to uniquely encode/decode each letter in the 26-letter alphabet. Mathematically, the number of decisions equals the base-2 logarithm of the number of symbols, e.g., $\log_2(26) = 4.7$. Fractional bits do not exist, so this is rounded up to 5.0.

Don't be put off by the use of logarithms in this definition. When the base-2 logarithm is used, it simply means "number of bits needed" to uniquely identify a certain quantity in the binary number system. The range of a number system such as base-10 is simply changed by shifting to a different scale. This can be seen from the table that follows. Logarithm base-2 rounded up to the next integer gives the number of bits required to scale base-10 numbers to base-2 binary numbers.

Decimal Number	Binary Equivalent	Scale Factor $\log_2$
0	0	–
1	1	0 rounded to 1.0
2	10	1 rounded to 2.0
3	11	1.59 rounded to 2.0
4	100	2.0 rounded to 3.0
5	101	2.33 rounded to 3.0
10	1010	3.33 rounded to 4.0
100	1100100	6.67 rounded to 7.0

This method of isolating English letters assumes every letter appears equally often in a message or English word. That is, it assumes uniformly random occurrence of letters of the alphabet. But, if we know that some letters in the English language occur more often than others, we can use this information to reduce the number of bits needed to encode/decode English words. We can compress the coded message, because common symbols contain less information than uncommon symbols. Uncommon or less frequent symbols require more bits to encode them, because they contain more information.

Shannon showed that information is related to surprise—more surprise means more uncertainty, and revealing or disclosing uncertainty is the essence of information. If the letter "s" appears more often than any other letter, then "s" carries *less* surprise and hence, *less* information. On the other hand, a rare occurrence of the letter "x" carries more surprise and therefore more information when revealed. Assuming the ith letter of the English alphabet appears with frequency p_i, the average information contained in the 26 English-language letters is calculated using Shannon's definition of *entropy* as follows:

$$I = -\sum_{i=1}^{26} p_i \log(p_i) \text{ bits}$$

For example, the frequencies of letters "a," "b," and "c," appearing in the Concise Oxford English Dictionary are 8.17%, 1.49%, and 2.78%, respectively.* The letter "e" is the most frequent (12.70%), and the letter "z" is the least frequent (0.074%). Using these percentages for p_i in the aforementioned equation yields average information content of 4.18, instead of 4.70. This says each symbol contains less than the maximum information possible because some of the information is already known—the letter "a" is five-and-a-half times more likely to appear in a word than the letter "b." The non-uniformity of frequencies p_i means the Concise Oxford English Dictionary can be compressed. However, 5 bits are still required to encode the letters because 4.18 bits of information requires 5 bits to represent every symbol.

Shannon postulated that information is *entropy*, which means random data contains more information than structured or redundant data. Stripping out randomness transforms disorder into order, revealing the intrinsic information hidden in the data. Thus, decoding reduces uncertainty to certainty. It also reduces information to zero. This seems at odds with common sense, but consider this: before data is decoded, it is indistinguishable from random noise. After it is decoded, its usefulness as new information vanishes and its information content drops to zero. But its meaning has risen to 100%. The signal has information before it is decoded and meaning after it is decoded.

---

* https://en.wikipedia.org/wiki/Letter_frequency

BENFORD'S LAW

Consider Benford's law used in forensics to detect financial fraud. It says that leading digits in real-world numerical data should obey a non-uniform *power law*, where the most frequent leading nonzero digit is "1" (30.1%), "2" (17.6%), ..., and the least frequent leading digit is "9" (4.60%).* We can use the frequency data in Table 2.1 to calculate the average information in the leading digits of a "Benford spreadsheet." An actual spreadsheet containing financial data too far from the Benford ideal is an indication that the spreadsheet may have been tampered with. The thief is unlikely to follow Benford's law while inserting fraudulent numbers in the spreadsheet.

An honest Benford spreadsheet contains approximately 2.88 bits of information. But if leading digits appear randomly with approximately the same frequency, the entropy will be closer to 3.48. In other words, an honest spreadsheet contains less information than a random spreadsheet. Shannon's prediction is a type of fingerprint that forensic experts use to detect tampering.

Processing of information content using much more sophisticated methods than given here, but based on the same principles of Shannon's information theory, have been successfully applied to cryptology and data compression since the 1940s. In fact, Shannon himself spent years working on cryptology for the US military during WWII. Secret codes obscure meaning by randomization. Compression removes redundancy or exploits non-uniformity to conserve bits. Shannon's information theory is the foundation of both applications.

TABLE 2.1 The Frequency of Leading Digits in Benford's Law Obeys a Power Law

Leading Digit	Frequency
1	30.1%
2	17.6%
3	12.5%
4	9.7%
5	7.9%
6	6.7%
7	5.8%
8	5.1%
9	4.6%

* https://en.wikipedia.org/wiki/Benford%27s_law

CHANNEL CAPACITY

Once Shannon realized that information is a form of entropy, he was in a position to quantify the amount of information that can be transmitted through any medium called a *channel*, in the presence of noise. In other words, he provided the theoretical basis for Hamming's code, but from an entirely theoretical angle. Shannon reasoned that channel capacity is the number of bits of information and noise that a medium can support. Thus, capacity, C, in terms of information bits is given by subtracting noise bits from the signal.

In terms of bits:

$$C = \log_2(\text{Signal}) - \log_2(\text{Noise})$$

Recall that Hamming defined Signal in terms of Information and Noise:

$$\text{Signal} = \text{Information} + \text{Noise}$$

Substituting this into the capacity equation:

$$C = \log_2(\text{Information} + \text{Noise}) - \log_2(\text{Noise})$$

$$= \log_2\big[(\text{Information} + \text{Noise})/\text{Noise}\big] = \log_2\big[1 + \text{Information}/\text{Noise}\big]$$

The term Information/Noise is usually called the "signal-to-noise ratio," S/N, and written as:

$$C = \log_2\big[1 + S/N\big]$$

Capacity is typically measured in bits per second, and sometimes equated with bandwidth. Thus, the upper limit of how much information can be transmitted over a medium of any kind is limited by the ratio of signal strength to noise. Suppose the signal-to-noise ratio equals 1.0. Then capacity $C = \log_2[2] = 1.0$.

Shannon's channel capacity made a profound impact on signal processing. It is a limit like the speed of light, beyond which nothing can travel. Given the Shannon limit C, the only parameter that can be improved is N. We want to improve channel capacity for a given noisy medium by reducing noise, N. The predominant way to do this is through clever and powerful coding, and decoding algorithms. Hamming devised the first method of noise reduction coding of the modern era and set off a burst of innovation in coding theory that continues to this day.

COMMENT

Richard Hamming retired from Bell Labs to pursue the pastoral pleasures of teaching at Stanford University, City College of New York, University of California at Irvine, Princeton University, and the Naval Postgraduate School. He correctly predicted that Bell Labs's budget for computing would eventually exceed 50%, when he left the labs in 1960.

In the spring of 1997, Hamming walked from his golf course home near the Pacific Ocean to the Naval Postgraduate School campus where eager students awaited his final lecture on "everything that is wrong with mathematics." He poked his head through the door to my office to let me know he was still alive. I used the opportunity to ask him why he hadn't retired earlier. He snapped back, "If I quit work, I will die." Less than one year later he died of a heart attack. That was January 1998.

Hamming's predictions were error-free.

Claude Shannon followed a similar path from research lab to academia until retirement in 1978. Although information theory was his legacy, his juggling, unicycling, and chess playing were also renowned among his peers. He was an incurable inventor who created a Roman numeral computer, juggling machine, robotic mouse that could traverse a maze, wearable computer used to beat the dealer in Las Vegas (with Edward O. Thorpe), and a Rubik's Cube solver.

His maxim was, "The enemy knows the system." He invented the system we call the Information Age.

The very idea that there is a fundamental unit of information and it can be digitized was revolutionary in the 1940s when analog radio was dominant and analog television was the next big thing. It went against the grain. After all, natural signals are continuous streams of information—not blocks or bursts of ones and zeros. It is the musical scale, the unbroken sound of wind, the hum of a busy city. It is the continuum of sight and sound blended together. We don't hear bits in a recording. We don't see bits in a photograph or movie.

One is tempted to compare information theory with quantum theory, because both are based on discrete quantities. The quantum jump bounded by Planck's constant is substituted for the on or off state of a bit. Nothing exists in between. Actions at the sub-atomic level happen in discrete jumps. Information in the signal exists or not, in discrete packets called bits. Both are somewhat ethereal, but fundamental at the same time.

Shannon and Hamming created a world made of bits when the world we sense around us appears analog. We cannot see or feel bits any more than we see or feel quantum jumps. Does information really exist in the form of bits or is information theory simply a fiction? This raises a major question, "How does information, in the form of bits, get captured, stored, transmitted, received, and interpreted in an analog world?"

CHAPTER 3

Elvis Has Left
the Building

G IGANTIC 12-FOOT ANTENNAS STRETCHED upward like huge elephant ears reaching to the stars over Barstow, California on Tuesday, November 28, 2017. They were searching the skies for hints of life onboard *Voyager I*—the first human-made object to cross the Heliopause and enter interstellar space. *Voyager* found its way past the reach of the solar winds on August 25, 2012, and sped outward under its own power since its last rocket burst in 1980. Now was time to order a small correction in its trajectory, which oddly was programmed to veer out of the planetary plane, heading north at an angle of 35 degrees or so. Its sister, *Voyager II*, was plunging southward at more than 45 degrees, as it too sped into outer space.* Both headed out of the solar system and out of the plane of the solar system.

The plutonium-powered thermoelectric generator onboard *Voyager I* still had enough power in 2012 to keep systems alive for perhaps another decade, but the small navigation rockets had been inactive since 1980— more than 37 years earlier! The radioactive generator provided enough juice to keep up communications, but the rockets may have been damaged or simply exhausted after the 13-billion-mile journey. Would the small altitudinal rockets still work? There was only one way to find out.

Project manager Suzanne Dodd and ground crew at JPL (Jet Propulsion Lab) in California signaled the spacecraft to execute an altitude correction

---

* https://voyager.jpl.nasa.gov/mission/science/planetary-voyage/

with a few millisecond puffs from the onboard rockets, and then waited nearly 40 hours for the return signal to confirm or deny the order. The engineers and scientists fell silent as anticipation filled the command and control room. At 13 billion miles from Earth, radio waves required 19 hours and 35 minutes for one-way travel to *Voyager I*, and another 19h:35m to return. It was a suspenseful wait.

After 40 years in space, the half-life decay of plutonium meant it produced less power than when *Voyager* launched in 1977. Over that 40 years, power declined from 470 watts to approximately 270 watts, or about one-half of its original level. The enormous distance from Earth further degrades effective power according to the inverse-square law that says intensity of light (and radio wave) diminishes inversely with the square of distance. Doubling the distance cuts intensity by a factor of four. The X-band and S-band transmitters onboard *Voyager I* need the equivalent of a 20-watt light bulb to operate. This is like shining a typical refrigerator light on a carton of ice cream from billions of miles away. Assuming it is even possible to see a 20-watt light bulb from the surface of the moon on a clear cloudless night, the same signal from 13 billion miles—200,000 times further—is 40,000,000,000 times fainter. Or if you prefer comparing *Voyager* with your home computer, consider this: the Wi-Fi router in your house typically uses approximately 6 watts to connect your smart phone and computer to the Internet. Picking up *Voyager*'s signal from deep space is more difficult than picking up your home's Wi-Fi signal from the *moon*. The signal received in 2017 was 0.1 billion billionth of a watt in strength, and transmitted data at 160 bits per second—about a million times slower than your home computer. But it worked!

Big antennas in the California desert are not big enough to resolve such a weak signal, so communications engineers use a clever signal-boosting technique called radio interferometry, invented in the 1950s by British scientist Roger Jennison (1922–2006). Extremely weak extraterrestrial signals are boosted by electronically linking together three downloading sites, each positioned approximately 1/3 of the way around earth—one in California, one in Madrid, Spain, and one in Canberra, Australia. The 120-degree separation means at least one site is in contact with spacecraft at any time of day, as the Earth rotates. More importantly, it also means the collection of antennas emulates one gigantic antenna equal to the size of the maximum separation between them. The *Deep Space Network* is equivalent to a very big, planet-spanning antenna.

But, 13 billion miles is still a long way for radio signals to travel. The information can be blotted out by solar flares, scattered by Earth's atmosphere, or simply too faint to be heard, reliably. Who knows what can happen to signals traveling such long distances? Back in the 1970s when *Voyager* was built, scientists and engineers knew enough about signals and noise to anticipate the signal-villains lurking in deep space. They were very clever back in those pre-Internet days, and prepared *Voyager* to deal with faint signals over a noisy channel. Their designs have survived in space for decades, and are expected to survive for many more years after *Voyager* leaves the solar system.

Forty hours after the signal to startup, the rockets returned with good news, the ground crew cheered and tension evaporated. They had achieved another "first" in space exploration. Elvis may have left the building, but he could still be heard singing from far away.

Space exploration was one of the earliest applications of Shannon's new theory of communication using bits in place of analog signals. His exciting new theories motivated invention and innovation, and the space program kicked off a revolution in how we communicate by bringing together extremely bright and talented scientists and engineers in one place at one time working on the same problems. It started with unmanned probes, and the most ambitious probes of them all: *Voyager I* and *II*. Follow-on transfer of technology from the *Voyager* project and its descendants created the robust communications infrastructure we enjoy, today. A handful of pioneers and a daring space program accelerated development of the signal so that connecting smart phones to the Internet is a common everyday experience. Thus, *Voyager I* not only began a long journey into outer space—it also began a long technological journey into our everyday lives.

INSIDE PROJECT VOYAGER

Robert McEliece (1942–) of Caltech (California Institute of Technology) relates those early days at JPL (Jet Propulsion Lab) when *Voyager* engineers faced the challenges of building a communication system that could process weak signals over a noisy channel from a traveling spacecraft a long way from home. He said, "The dramatic photographs of Mercury, Venus, Mars, Jupiter, Saturn, Uranus, and Neptune transmitted by spacecraft with romantic names like *Mariner, Voyager, Viking,* etc. over distances of hundreds of millions, even billions, of miles, have made these planets, which were previously known to us only as fuzzy telescopic images in textbooks, as real to us in the 1990s as, say, the Himalayas, the Sahara Desert, or Antarctica."* He credits the Reed–Solomon codes as being a "part of the communications technology of planetary exploration, almost from the beginning." The "beginning," for McEliece, traces back to the early 1970s, but the Reed–Solomon code goes back even further. In a landmark paper in 1960, Irving Reed and Gustave Solomon explain how to encode information such that it can be transmitted over large distances or stored for long periods of time and retrieved intact, even if it contains errors. The Reed–Solomon code self-corrects and is especially impervious to bursts of noise that obliterate multiple bits of information.†

Reed–Solomon codes were deployed in *Voyager* as well as other early spacecraft. It is largely responsible for the 40-year success of transmission between Earth and *Voyager* 13 billion miles away. For decades, the Reed–Solomon code protected QR bar codes, CD and DVD recordings, as well as storage products underlying cloud computing and big data.

The Reed–Solomon code was not an instant success. In 2000, Reed reflected on his work,

> For years after its publication the Reed–Solomon code was viewed as interesting mathematics and little else. It simply did not appear to be practical with the computing capability of the day. Even in the mid-60s, when people at JPL began to build and fly spacecraft with error-correction coding, they turned not to the Reed–Solomon code but to the more straightforward but less powerful Reed–Muller code. Such was the case for the next decade. However, in the years since the late 1970s, concurrent with the development of more powerful computers and more efficient decoding architectures, such as that of Berlekamp, the Reed–Solomon code has been widely used in industrial and consumer electronic devices. At present billions of dollars in modern technology, the compact disc memories, digital communications, etc. depends on ideas

---

* McEliece, Robert and Laif Swanson (1993). Reed–Solomon Codes and the Exploration of the Solar System (20 Aug. 1993). https://trs.jpl.nasa.gov/bitstream/handle/2014/34531/94-0881. pdf?sequence=1

† Reed, Irving S. and Gustave Solomon (1960). Polynomial Codes over Certain Finite Fields. *Journal of the Society for Industrial and Applied Mathematics (SIAM)*, 8(2), pp. 300–304. doi:10.1137/0108018.

that stem from the original work of Solomon and myself almost 34 years ago.*

The 1970s technology of *Voyager* limited engineer's design options. Computing and electrical circuits were primitive and bulky. One of the earliest decoders used to process spacecraft signals was described as "a big monster filling a rack."† The designs had to be modest in terms of hardware, software, and power consumption. Simple designs were preferred over complex and bulky designs.

The basic idea was to translate raw data into a code that could be checked for errors using various forms of redundancy. For example, a simple triple-redundant code uses majority voting to detect and correct errors. Suppose a message from a spacecraft sends the first letter of the English alphabet to Earth as "a," but along the way it encounters noise and is changed to "#," an error. How does Earth know it is an error, and how might it be corrected? Triple-redundant coding improves the reliability of messaging by sending three copies, instead of one. Thus, the spacecraft sends "aaa" instead, and when Earth receives "#aa" it decodes this as "a," using majority voting.

As the signal becomes fainter and buried deeper in noise, the Hamming code becomes less capable. Spacecraft communications, for example, often encounter long bursts of noise that obliterate long sequences of code words. Greater redundancy and more powerful codes are required to overcome harsh environments. One technique employs a two-level hierarchy of encode/decode algorithms to defeat noise.

McEliece credits G. David Forney (1940–) with suggesting that *Voyager* incorporate a two-level hierarchical communication protocol whereby the outer code corrects errors made by the inner code. So, in the previous example of a triple-redundant code, if the inner code received "#aa," the outer code would detect and correct the received message. In this simple example, the outer code detects the "#" as an error, and replaces it with "a," after voting.

A Ph.D. student of Andrew J. Viterbi (1935–2016), Joseph P. Odenwalder (1941–) recommended a convolutional code processed by Viterbi's

* Reed, I.S. (2000). A Brief History of the Development of Error Correcting Codes. *Computers and Mathematics with Applications*, 39, pp. 89–93. https://ac.els-cdn.com/S0898122100001127/1-s2.0-S0898122100001127-main.pdf?_tid=9f4c0fae-96dd-4988-bfc7-d2872c0b7c8c&acdnat=152523259 0_631586c913ac4297d3f53922f725ece2

† Forney, G. David (2005). The Viterbi Algorithm: A Personal History (29 April 2005). https://arxiv.org/pdf/cs/0504020v2.pdf

algorithm as the inner code, and the Reed–Solomon block code as the outer code to handle error detection and correction. This combination would have a lasting effect on the entire field of communication. David Forney writes, "Andrew J. Viterbi is rightly celebrated as one of the leading communications engineers and theorists of the twentieth century."[*] Viterbi developed his algorithm after finding information theory difficult to teach, so he built his own tools based on his own interpretation of information theory. He thought his "tools" had no practical value, but they helped students understand information theory concepts and algorithms. In fact, they were not formally published in refereed journals for many years after their invention in 1967. The Viterbi algorithm is described in much greater detail in Chapter 8.

Meanwhile, Viterbi, Qualcomm cofounder Irwin Jacobs (1933–), and UCLA professor Len Kleinrock cofounded Linkabit Corporation in 1968 to provide a new breed of information coding algorithms to customers like the Voyager project. Viterbi and Jacobs went on to cofound Qualcomm and devise the CDMA (Code-Division Multiple Access) protocol for cellular communication that would revolutionize smart phone technology. Len Kleinrock would become one of the founding pioneers of the packet-switched Internet. See Chapter 5.

As the size of images transmitted back to Earth from spacecraft like *Mariner* (Mars) and *Voyager* became larger, engineers turned to compression algorithms to reduce storage and transmission costs. But compression is extremely sensitive to single-bit errors, which occurred in about five bits per one thousand bits received. This seems rather innocuous, but the 5:1000 error rate disproportionately impacts error detection and correction of compressed signals. This is where the outer code suggested by Forney comes to the rescue.

The multi-error-correcting Reed–Solomon code was used for the first time in deep space exploration in the spectacularly successful Voyager mission, which began in the summer of 1977 with the launch of twin spacecraft (*Voyager I* and *Voyager II*) from Cape Kennedy. The raw data of the *Voyager* imaging hardware produces three 800×800 pixel images of 8-bits per pixel to take low-resolution color photos. Thus, 15,360,000 bits have to be coded and sent to Earth. Robert F. Rice of JPL devised a compression algorithm that compressed planetary images by a factor of 2.5. But it was sensitive to errors—a perfect challenge for the Reed–Solomon (RS) self-correcting algorithm. The problem was solved using a ground-based RS(255, 223)

---

[*] Ibid., Forney.

decoding algorithm built by Charles R. Lahmeyer. Every image from *Voyager* is cut into blocks of 255 bits each, with 223 bits containing image pixels and 32 bits of redundancy capable of correcting up to 16 errors. This combination of compressing and coding for errors has been phenomenally successful. So successful, in fact, that it has been copied hundreds of times in hundreds of consumer products like CDs and DVDs.

HOW REED MET SOLOMON

Irving S. Reed (1923–2012) knew nothing about error-correcting codes as a Caltech student in the 1950s, but he repeatedly ran into some of the early pioneers in reliable communication and information theory while in college and later while working. He served on the same US Navy destroyer as information coding pioneer David A. Huffman (1925–1999) during WWII. The GI Bill sent him to Caltech where he met David E. Muller (1924–2008), with whom he reunited later to implement the Reed–Muller code. Following his mathematics studies, he went to work for Northrop Aircraft Corporation, noting that they had a good library because of a joint partnership with Caltech's library. This is where Reed stumbled onto Shannon's earliest papers, circa 1949, on information theory and the concept of communication channels with limited signal capacity. If errors were introduced via noise, capacity dropped. Hamming showed how to use redundancy to compensate for errors. Exactly how much redundancy is needed to communicate from 13 billion miles?

College pal Muller and Reed continued to collaborate after Muller went to the University of Illinois and Reed went to Northrop. Reed recalls, "In a notation of his own invention, Dave Muller described a new error-correction code in his report on logic design. His codes were based on what he called a *Boolean Net Function*, which I didn't have the energy at the time to understand. However, I decided what he must have had in mind were what are called multinomials over a Boolean field, the finite field of two elements 0 and 1."[*] This was a conceptual breakthrough for Reed. The idea clicked because of his mathematical training in an obscure branch of mathematics called Galois field theory. Mathematicians abbreviated Galois field theory over binary numbers as GF(2).

My idea of using polynomials over the primitive finite field GF(2) of two elements was very fruitful. By constraining the maximum degree of these multinomials over N variables I managed

---

[*] Ibid., Reed.

to construct an error-correcting code, which was equivalent to the codes Muller had found. The algebraic structure imposed on these multinomials made it possible for me to find a decoding algorithm for these codes, which is now called majority-logic decoding. Also, I demonstrated that these codes are group codes. They are a group or vector space with respect to vector addition over GF(2).

GF(2) math is and was so obscure that only mathematicians understood it at the time. Reed lamented, "For well over 100 years mathematicians looked upon Galois fields as elegant mathematics but of no practical value. It was my idea to use the elements of a finite field as an alphabet to use symbols rather than bits, e.g., half-bytes or bytes for the symbols. This was the beginning of the thought process that led ultimately to the Reed–Solomon codes." As it turned out, Galois field theory was perfect for building self-correcting codes out of streams of bits, because it provided a rigorous basis, and it came at just the right time in history when digital met communication signals and binary computers were on the verge of exponential improvement. Innovation is often the merger of something old with something new, and the Reed–Solomon code perfectly combined old Galois field theory with the new emerging field of digital communications.

When Gustave Solomon (1930–1996) joined Reed's work group in early 1958, Reed knew exactly what to do with him. He showed his work on coding using GF(2) and together they proved the theorems necessary to establish the Reed–Solomon (RS) algorithm as solid science. The 5-page paper, "Polynomial Codes Over Certain Finite Fields," appeared in the Journal of the Society of Industrial and Applied Mathematics (SIAM), in June 1960. And it was ignored for most of the decade. One might say that Reed and Solomon built a (finite) field, and nobody came.

In 1999 Stephen Wicker and Vijay Bhargava wrote,

On January 21, 1959, Irving Reed and Gus Solomon submitted a paper to the Journal of the Society for Industrial and Applied Mathematics. In June of 1960 the paper was published: five pages under the rather unpretentious title "Polynomial Codes over Certain Finite Fields." This paper described a new class of error-correcting codes that are now called Reed–Solomon codes. In the decades since their discovery, Reed–Solomon codes have enjoyed countless applications from compact disc players in living rooms all over the planet to spacecraft that are now well beyond the orbit of Pluto. Reed–Solomon codes have been an integral part of the telecommunications revolution in the last half of the twentieth century.* This sole publication started a two-decade long series of innovations that culminated in the pervasive application of Reed–Solomon to perfecting the signal.

McEliece writes in praise of Solomon, "Gustave Solomon, world renowned coding theorist, legendary character, and beloved friend and teacher to many members of the Information Theory Society, died at his home in Beverly Hills, California, on January 31, 1996."† He was a "legendary character" because of his love of music, singing, and acting. He studied piano and composed many songs while a teenager. He was a voice coach to hundreds of students, including professional singers, actors, and theatrical performers. He was also one of the few people in the world that understood the work of a mathematical prodigy named Évariste Galois.

THE BAD BOY OF MATH

Évariste Galois (1811–1832) was convinced he was going to die the next day. He pushed the dread from his mind as a torrent of ideas poured onto the paper before him. Even though he was obsessed with documenting his mathematical ideas before his inevitable death, he could not stop his mind from sifting through his brief 20 years of life. Galois recalled an earlier time spent with his mother as she home-schooled him until he was 12 years old. These were the best 12 years of his life. He was not bitter, but life went mostly downhill after those warm and secure days with his mother. Why do condemned men think of their mothers when they are about to die?

This was not the first time he was thrown into prison for behaving badly. It was, however, the last time, because certain death awaited his release. Still, he kept on writing throughout the night, replacing the candles as they burned down, and asking the guards for more paper and ink. His dank cell was typical of French revolutionary prisons—a completely inhumane place to store uncooperative malcontents while they awaited an

---

* Wicker, Stephen B. and Vijay K. Bhargava (1999). An Introduction to Reed–Solomon Codes, Chapter 1. http://catalogimages.wiley.com/images/db/pdf/0780353919.excerpt.pdf
† http://backup.itsoc.org/publications/nltr/96_jun/01obi.pdf

arbitrary fate. The whole system stunk more than his cell. Yet, he forced himself to think, write, think some more, and write some more. It was an act of desperation.

His thoughts wandered back and forth from dread to his new theory of mathematical fields. Somehow he had become a rebellious republican—part of the rabble—as the French Revolution raged on around him. Sometimes he rebelled along with the rabble, but mostly he developed his mathematical theory in isolation. A major uprising in 1830 set the stage for his poor condition. Another uprising in 1832 became material for Victor Hugo's book, *Les Misérables*. Galois was living out *Les Misérables*. He was collateral damage.

He pressed on through the night. Inventing *field theory*—a theory that explained how numbers and arithmetic operations formed fields— especially finite fields. When two numbers are combined by addition, for example, the sum can land in the same field or not, depending on how the field is defined. For example, $2 + 3 = 5$. Elements 2, 3, and 5 belong to the same set of integers or what Galois called a *field*. So too does the product of 2 times 3 or 6, but 2/3 does not belong, because 0.6666... is a real number and not an integer. A finite field, Galois furiously wrote, is a set of numbers and the operations that produce results in the *same* field.

Additionally, a finite field must have a finite number of elements. The countable integers won't do, because there are an infinite number of integers. As far as Galois was concerned, a finite number of numbers would do. In fact, binary numbers—called *bits* over 100 years later—would do very well, indeed, because operations on bits are so much simpler. The set of numbers 0, 1, 2, 3, 4, 5, 6, and 7 can be expressed as 3-bit strings 000, 001, 010, 011, 100, 101, 110, 111. Adding and subtracting them in a finite field was simple, too. The exclusive OR operation, XOR, replaces both addition and subtraction. The result of an XOR is always zero, unless the two bits differ. Therefore, 1 XOR 1 is zero just like 0 XOR 0, but 1 XOR 0 is 1. So is 0 XOR 1.

Galois arithmetic is incredibly simple—so simple a machine can add and subtract binary numbers by XOR operations on pairs. But it is easy to get confused so I will attempt to do as much arithmetic as possible in the familiar decimal system, except where it is entirely necessary!

The manuscript pages piled up in front of him as the unrelenting tower clock counted down to his eventual doom. A 12-hour clock forms a set of integers zero (a.k.a. 12 midnight) to 11, he thought. Adding an hour to any time, zero to 11, produced an hour number in the same field: 0 (a.k.a. 12) to 11. For example, $2 + 3 = 5$ o'clock. But, what about adding 10 hours to a 12-hour clock? Starting from 3 o'clock in the morning, adding 10 hours causes the hour hand of the tower clock to "wrap around" to 1 pm the next day. And 1 is still within the same field as 3 and 5. He would be dead by then. The thought pushed him to write even faster.

A finite field of integers is easily formed under multiplication and division by taking the remainder and discarding the divisor. Glancing at the tower clock Galois noted that it would soon be 4 o'clock in the morning. Dividing by 2 hours rewound the hour hand back to 2 o'clock. Dividing by 3 hours, however, rewound the hour hand back to 1 o'clock, because 3 divides 4 by one, with a remainder of 1. If the remainder is kept and the divisor thrown away, the operation of division forms a finite field over the set of integers zero to 11. To maintain a finite field, only the remainder after division matters. Similarly, multiplying 3 o'clock by 5 produces 3 instead of 15, because 15 is beyond the finite field. But $15/12 = 3$, gives a number in the finite field so reducing 15 to 3 keeps multiplication in the field. Multiplication also wraps around. The numbers in the hour hand of the tower clock form a finite field.

The wrap-around feature is even simpler in binary. Adding $4 + 5$ equals $(100) + (101)$ using 3-bit strings. But $4 + 5 = 9$, which is outside of the field. The XOR operation produces a result within the field, (001). That is, $4 + 5 = 1$, over $GF(2^3)$. Galois was pushing the limits of his mathematical contemporaries as he documented new concepts like binary numbers, finite fields, and operations that wrapped around. But he had very little success proving his point during his brief lifetime.

It is 4 am and he begins to flashback. His fortunes steadily declined after leaving home for the same boarding school attended by Robespierre, Voltaire, and Victor Hugo. He was a lackluster student until discovering the works of Legendre, the famous French mathematician. Even though he was expelled from school, things began to look up for a brief period of time as he consumed the works of the great mathematicians. He made several attempts to enter university, and was refused, time after time. Then his father, a prominent man of the community, killed himself. Galois went into a tailspin, but kept working on finite fields, writing and submitting papers to journals for publication. And, suffering more rejection.

For 3 years his pioneering papers on Galois field theory were repeatedly panned. His ideas were simply too advanced for the era, and his writings too dense to be easily understood. For example, he wrote that finite fields could also be formed by mathematical equations known as polynomials—what Reed called multinomials over a century later. A polynomial like $x^2 + x + 1$ and operations like multiplication and division of polynomials like $(x^3 + x^2 + x + 1)/(x^2 + x + 1)$ also form finite fields. Even more interesting for 1830s France, these polynomials can be defined for very elementary fields that would eventually be called $GF(2^n)$, because the elements of the field are binary numbers containing n bits. That is, Galois formulated a theory based on binary numbers over a century before binary computers were invented.

The reality of impending death kept crowding out his thoughts, as he wrote notes in the margins of his pioneering mathematical treatise. Comments about the daughter of the prison physician named Stephanie-Felice du Motel appear in the columns next to polynomials over $GF(2^n)$. She had rebuffed his advances, but he could not erase her from his tormented mind. He could also not erase the impending duel with Perscheux d'Herbinville, who patiently awaited his release.

The night faded into a gray soup as Galois finished writing. He was released and at dawn on May 30, 1832 faced d'Herbinville in a duel. His nemesis promptly put a bullet in his abdomen and left him to die on the ground ripe with spring grass and yellow flowers. Collected by a passerby and taken to a hospital, Galois died the next day. Death was as painful for Galois as his life.

Galois field theory was published in 1846, 14 years after his death. It went unnoticed for most of the next 100 years. Digital computing, digital signal processing, and self-correcting codes in support of spacecraft traveling through deep space 13 billion miles from the sun had to be invented before Galois field theory became an essential part of forming, transmitting, and receiving signals. The RS algorithm is based on the deep mathematics invented by Évariste Galois over a century earlier. So are many other algorithms essential to computing and transmitting signals.

GALOIS FIELDS AS FEEDBACK-SHIFT REGISTERS

One of the amazing fallouts from Galois theory is how compatible it is with digital hardware. By digital, I mean binary. Galois fields are defined over binary numbers processed by feedback-shift registers inside computing and signal transmitting machines. A shift register is exactly what its name implies—it shifts bits left or right, which corresponds with multiplication and division in binary. Thus, operations like addition, subtraction, multiplication, and division are all reduced to a series of shifts. More important, and exquisitely, Galois field *polynomials* are divided by shifting just like ordinary numbers are divided by long division.

Binary division can be expressed as division of Galois polynomials such as $(x^3 + x^2 - x + 1)/(x^2 + x + 1)$ by shifting bits through a shift register that shifts and performs only XOR operations. No need for the laborious long division done by human hand. Instead, the properties of Galois fields make long division trivial. Galois field theory became the basis of signal processing in the twentieth century because it simplified arithmetic on binary numbers represented as Galois polynomials. It is perhaps one of the most profound recombinant innovations of the Information Age, because it enabled self-correcting codes.

Self-correcting codes are based on the remainder left over after division. Fast and efficient division of binary numbers expressed as Galois polynomials is the key to modern signal processing.

SELF-CORRECTING CODES (ADVANCED)

Galois field theory was largely forgotten for decades after his death. Curiously, a very small handful of mathematicians began to show interest in applied Galois field theory following Hamming's amazing code. Throughout the 1950s, mathematicians gradually re-invented field theory and applied it to the new discipline of error-correcting code design. These advances culminated in the publication of a paper by W. Wesley Peterson (1924–2009) at the University of Hawaii in 1961. Peterson applied binary field theory to binary data in a computer, thus linking theory and application. The idea is simple, in hindsight: let the redundant checking bits be the remainder obtained by dividing the information bits by a GF(2) polynomial. Reverse the process at the receiving end and compare. If remainders match, there is no error. This algorithm became known as a *cyclic redundant check* (CRC).

Reed–Solomon and subsequent error detection and correction algorithms are all different forms of CRC codes. What makes them special and successful is they are founded on solid mathematical ground because of Galois and inspired mathematicians that followed. The key is recognizing that binary numbers can be represented as binary polynomials over a Galois field, and that dividing one polynomial by another produces a remainder polynomial that checks on the information polynomial. For example, $195/33 = 5$ with a remainder of 30. Thus, 30 is a redundancy check on the correctness of 195. The decimal numbers 195 and 33 can also be represented by GF(2) polynomials that are amenable to shift register processing.

A rigorous explanation of Galois field theory and the Reed–Solomon code is beyond the scope of this book, but the concepts are easily explained by analogy using grade-school arithmetic. Recall that the basis of self-correction is redundancy. But we don't want too much redundancy because it increases the size of the signal and larger signals provide more opportunity for errors. That is, at some point, errors creep into redundancy, itself, defeating its purpose. So, one goal of signal coding is to keep error-correcting redundancy at a minimum. Another goal is to enable rapid coding and decoding, which bears on transmission bandwidth.

Consider a signal based on a finite field {0, 1, 2, 3, 4, 5, 6, 7}. That is, the only acceptable symbols for transmission are the digits 0, 1, 2, 3, 4, 5, 6, and 7, which can be represented by three bits, each. Suppose a message M is encoded and sent as signal T over a noisy channel (such as air or empty space), and received as (potentially scrambled signal) R:

M: the message containing one or more of the eight symbols

T: the message and its remainder after division by 33

R: the signal that is received at the other end

E: errors in the received signal. $R = T + E$

More formally, R is a signal containing M and one or more errors, E. Thus, $R = T + E$. The received signal contains the correct message, and possibly errors that must be detected and corrected. The trick is to separate out the errors, using Galois field encoding and decoding. If we are clever enough, we can encode M into T such that we can separate out the error E from the received signal at the other end.

For example, let the intended message be {1234}. Division by 33 yields a remainder of 13. If we encode and transmit both {1234} and 13, the receiver can verify that no error has occurred if it also divides by 33 and obtains $r = 13$ as a remainder. The long division table that follows illustrates this. The result of 1234/33 is 37 with a remainder of 13. Since we only care about the remainder, we discard 37. Mathematically, obtaining a remainder after integer division is called modulo arithmetic and its operation is the **mod** operation. Therefore, 1234 **mod** 33 is 37. The following tables show how grade-school long division yields the **mod** operation on 1234.

Result				3	7	r13
33	1	2	3	4		
		9	9			
		2	4	4		
		2	3	1		
			1	3		

Now, suppose an error occurs so that the received message is {1224} instead of {1234}. The receiver divides by 33 as before, but also notes the discrepancy in remainder and intermediate results of long division. The next table shows the arithmetic for obtaining the remainder as well as intermediate results.

Result				3	7	r3
33	1	2	2	4		
		9	9			
		2	3	4		
		2	3	1		
			0	3		

The first thing we notice is that the remainder $r = 3$ is not 13. Therefore, an error must have occurred, but where? The intermediate results of long division are identical except for the final row of the table containing the results of long division, at row 4. Specifically, a 3 appears in row 4, column 4, instead of 4. The discrepancy appears in row 4, where 234 should be 244, instead. This suggests that an error occurred in column 4, corresponding with the second 2 in {1224}. Furthermore, $4 - 3 = 1$, so the second 2 in {1224} must be off by one. We can correct this error by adding 1 to get the correct signal {12(2 + 1)4} -> {1234}.

Galois, Peterson, Reed, and Solomon took this concept one giant step for mankind further by expressing the elements, M and T of the finite field, as polynomials over a binary finite field of polynomials, instead of simple integers. So, the divisor becomes $x^2 + 3x + 2$, and the message {1234} becomes $M(x) = x^5 + 2x^4 + 3x^3 + 4x^2$, leaving room at the tail end for the remainder, $(4x + 0)$. The following table shows that $T(x) = M(x) + (4x + 0)$ is exactly divisible by $x^2 + 3x + 2$, with a remainder of zero.

Result	x^3	x^2	2x		r4x
$x^2 + 3x + 2$	x^5	$2x^4$	$3x^3$	$4x^2$	4x
	x^5	$3x^4$	$2x^3$		
		x^4	x^3	$4x^2$	
		x^4	$3x^3$	$2x^2$	
			$2x^3$	$6x^2$	4x
			$2x^3$	$6x^2$	4x
					0

The message $M(x)$ is encoded as $T(x)$, transmitted, and decoded into $R(x)$. Since the remainder is zero, $R(x)$ exactly equals $M(x)$. Thus, the correct signal is sent and received. The observant reader will notice a peculiarity in the long division table, above. For example, $2x^4$ minus $3x^4$ is x^4, and $4x^2$ minus $2x^2$ is $6x^2$. Why? The arithmetic in $GF(2^3)$ is different than in decimal, because addition and subtraction are both the same in $GF(2^3)$. In fact, they are XOR operations on polynomials just like XOR on binary numbers. Given eight symbols, 0, 1, 2, 3, 4, 5, 6, and 7, over binary field $GF(2^3)$, each symbol is coded as a 3-bit number. Recall that 2 is (010), 3 is (011), 4 is (100), and 6 is (110). Addition is replaced by XOR which means a XOR b = 1 if a and b differ, and 0, otherwise.

$2x^4$ minus $3x^4$ becomes $(010)x^4$ XOR $(011)x^4 = (001)x^4$, which is 1x, and $4x^2$ minus $2x^2$ becomes $6x^2$, because (100) XOR (010) is (110) = 6. The 3-bit binary numbers and XOR operations form a $GF(8)$ finite field in Galois theory. As an additional bonus, the XOR operation is an extremely simple electronic circuit to build. It is also much easier to perform division in $GF(8)$ than decimal using simple hardware shift registers. But this is another story that is shortened into this:

*The XOR operation in $GF(2)$ replaces the **mod** operation in grade school arithmetic.*

Suppose the incorrect message $R(x) = x^5 + 2x^4 + 2x^3 + 4x^2 + 4x$ is received, instead. The receiver performs division as before, and if the remainder is nonzero, an error has crept into the signal. We can detect and correct the error as before by noticing where the discrepancy in division first occurs. In this case, the zero in row 4, column 4 should be 1. To correct the error, we solve the $GF(2)$ equation: $e + 0 = (001)$. Thus, $e = (000)$ XOR $(001) = (001)$. The correction is obtained by "adding" e to the signal: correction = (010) XOR $(001) = (011)$, which is 3. Thus, the correct signal is {1234} as it should be.

Result	x^3	x^2	$3x$		$r7x^2+2x$
x^2+3x+2	x^5	$2x^4$	$2x^3$	$4x^2$	$4x$
	x^5	$3x^4$	$2x^3$		
		x^4	$0x^3$	$4x^2$	
		x^4	$3x^3$	$2x^2$	
			$3x^3$	$6x^2$	$4x$
			$3x^3$	$9x^2$	$6x$
				$7x^2$	$2x$

The Reed–Solomon code languished for nearly a decade because it lacked an efficient decoding algorithm. Forney's decoding algorithm required the solution to a set of simultaneous equations, which limited its practical application. Unlike the Hamming code described earlier, the checking bits in the Reed–Solomon code cover all information bits, not just selected and overlapping bits. This indiscriminant coverage makes decoding via syndromes much more difficult and computationally expensive to perform, even for a fast computer. The error-correcting block at the end of the signal does not have the cross-reference property of a Hamming code. Only the solution to many simultaneous equations is capable of sorting out the position of error bits.

Fortunately, in 1967 Elwyn Berlekamp (1940–) demonstrated an efficient decoding algorithm for Reed–Solomon codes. His algorithm efficiently decodes dozens of errors at a time—a big breakthrough that stimulated others to study Reed–Solomon codes in earnest. In 1968, Massey (1934–2013) demonstrated a hardware shift register-based decoding Berlekamp algorithm that is now commonly referred to as the Berlekamp–Massey algorithm. These innovations brought the Reed–Solomon code back to life, and the rest is history.

The Forney-inspired Viterbi decoding algorithm will be described in more detail in Chapter 8, because in a strange twist of fate, the Viterbi algorithm has become more modern as decades of innovation improved on CRC codes in general, and the Reed–Solomon code in particular. As it turns out, Viterbi was way ahead of his time just like Galois.

COMMENT

The Reed–Solomon algorithm detects and corrects up to e errors if the remainder contains 2e bits. The Voyager mission used 255-bit codes with 32-bit remainders, in what became a standard RS(255, 223) code in subsequent consumer products like DVDs. The RS(255, 223) code assigns

223 bits to the message, and 32 bits to the error-correcting remainder. Thus, RS(255, 223) can correct up to 16 errors. Additionally, each symbol in this code is 8 bits, so that up to 16 of the 32 symbols (including the remainder bits) can be corrected. The 32 error-correction bits consume 12.5% of the information bits in an RS(255, 223) code. This is far more efficient than triple redundancy or Hamming codes. What this means in practice is that up to 16 errors can be detected and corrected for the price of a 12.5% reduction in bandwidth. This is a small price to pay for rescuing a signal from noise.

Voyager had very limited memory, so it was impractical to store tables like we have shown here. Additionally, long division is too inefficient in general, so extremely clever mathematical equations for finding and correcting errors are used in place of tables. The Berlekamp–Massey algorithm is commonly used in practical applications. More recently, French professor Claude Berrou (1951–) proposed faster coding algorithms called *turbo codes* to replace the RS code in cellular communications (since G3), hard disk drives (since 2012), and WiMax (IEEE 802.16).* Even more recently, other codes have been proposed that exploit 5G communication standards. For example, the polar code exploits the MIMO standard in 5G that provides multiple parallel channels to increase bandwidth. Turbo and polar codes come the closest to Shannon's theoretical limit of channel capacity over a noisy channel.

The RS code still lives on in the form of the QR bar code stamped on almost all goods sold at retail stores. Its durability is a tribute to the ingenuity of Reed and Solomon, but it is likely to fade as new technologies like 5G take over.

Reed–Solomon codes are often called BCH codes after academic advisor Raj Bose (1901–1987), his Ph.D. student D. K. Ray-Chaudhuri (1933–), and Alexis Hocquenghem (1908–1990) independently discovered the power of GF(2) polynomials to encode and decode noisy signals using the idea of a cyclic redundant check (CRC). There is no evidence that Reed and Solomon were aware of the work of BCH or that BCH inventors were aware of the work of Reed and Solomon.

William Wesley Peterson (1924–2009) is also generally credited with designing the first error-correcting codes using the same ideas of CRC.

---

* Berrou, C., A. Glavieux, and P. Thitimajshima (1993). Near Shannon Limit Error-Correcting Coding and Decoding: Turbo Codes. *IEEE Proceedings of the International Conference on Communications*, Geneva, Switzerland, May 1993 (ICC'93), pp. 1064–1070.

Peterson was awarded the Japan Prize in 1999 and the Claude E. Shannon Award in 1981 for contributions to information theory and coding in the late 1950s and early 1960s, including authoring a number of standard textbooks on information coding. Peterson's CRC algorithm was incorporated into Intel processors as the CRC32 instruction for correcting data transmission errors.

Most of the pioneers that brought us reliable communication technology underlying modern communications have passed away or retired. It is interesting to note that the entire communications industry operating today came from a handful of organizations and people working in an arcane and infrequently recognized discipline. While most people have heard of *Voyager*, own a smart phone, use Wi-Fi every day, and depend on QR bar codes, few have heard of the pioneers whose work made it all possible. And yet great companies like Qualcomm remain today, extending the results of these pioneers.

Descendants of the Forney and Viterbi algorithms for decoding Reed–Solomon codes paved the road to early methods of locating and correcting errors, but it was not the only path to error correction. The Viterbi algorithm proposed by Andrew Viterbi in 1967 was an option based on dynamic programming that over the next 40 years would prove to be more fruitful as an approach to decoding, especially as computational power increased and spectrum became widely available. Forney paid tribute to the Viterbi algorithm in 2005 when he said,

> The Viterbi algorithm has been tremendously important in communications. For moderately complex (not capacity-approaching) codes, it has proved to yield the best tradeoff between performance and complexity both on power-limited channels, such as space channels, and on bandwidth-limited channels, such as voice band telephone lines. In practice, in these regimes it has clearly outstripped its earlier rivals, such as sequential decoding and algebraic decoding.[6]

The importance of the Viterbi algorithm to modern coding theory and practice will be revisited in Chapter 8, where it is shown to be a special case of a much more powerful technique called Markov modeling. But first, additional innovations had to fall into place before advanced encoding/decoding algorithms were made practical by advanced hardware technology and clever mathematics.

CHAPTER 4

Butterflies and Bits

I WAS LOOKING FOR A gasoline station along Central Expressway in Mountain View, California on a spring day in 1967 when I saw a large sign in front of a giant aluminum ball next to a mysterious building. I swerved over to the right lane and exited at the next stoplight, contemplating how to reach the aluminum sphere without causing an accident. GPS navigation was 50 years into the future, so I backtracked by old-fashioned pilotage. Eventually, I located the giant ball, its dull gray paint hiding a secret, no doubt. I pulled into the parking lot and found ample parking spaces.

The spring of 1967 was a time of political turmoil, but also a time of great opportunity. The CMOS revolution was about to take over and turn Santa Clara Valley into Silicon Valley. A 13-year-old Bill Gates was enrolled in Lakeside School in 1967, where the Mother's Club had raised money to purchase an ASR-33 teletypewriter and computer time on a DEC PDP-10 owned by General Electric Timesharing Corporation. Microsoft Corporation would benefit from his experience a decade later. In another year, semiconductor pioneers Robert Noyce and Gordon Moore would cofound Intel Corporation for the purpose of producing dynamic RAM chips for IBM computers. Within yet another year, Ken Thomson and Dennis Ritchie would begin working on version 1.0 of Unix—the foundation of all modern smart phone operating systems and the future basis of Apple Computer's MacOS. Still further out, the precursor of the Internet—ARPANet—was still just an idea rattling around the halls of the Pentagon.

There was noticeably very little traffic on the broad expressway running through the jungle of industrial buildings with legendary names and products to come. Far from being Masters of the Universe, the buildings looked sparse and unimpressive to me. I parked in one of the many open spaces and made my way to the nondescript building apparently holding up the giant ball. The war in Vietnam beckoned to unemployed college dropouts with no military draft deferment, so I hastened into the building through a door that looked like the servant's entrance. Brushing my long hair out of my eyes, I eagerly asked the receptionist what kind of engineers they wanted. She escorted me into another office where I was interviewed and immediately hired. It was quick but not easy. Questions had to be answered. "Do you know what a Fourier Transform is?", "How would you find the roots of a polynomial on a computer?", "What programming languages do you know?"

Fortunately, I had worked my way through undergraduate school as an operator of a primitive vacuum tube computer called the Alwac-3E. I knew ALGOL and Fortran, and I could perform Fourier Transforms for co-eds at parties. I was the right guy for this job, whatever it was. I ran back to my car and started looking for a place to live. My life oscillated between going to school until I ran out of money, and going to work until I had enough money to go to school. This was the work-for-food phase.

OSCILLATING SIGNALS

I was put into an office with John Morton—another graduate of Oregon State University—and handed a coding sheet. The job was to digitally analyze signals from top-secret surveillance probes bordering the Soviet Union. This is called SIGINT, or Signal Intelligence, in the business. All kinds of information can be gleaned from all kinds of signals scavenged from listening posts around the globe. Somehow this longhaired hippie had stumbled into a top-secret job and handed the keys to the kingdom simply because I knew something about the Fourier Transform. As it turned out, few people in 1967 knew Fourier Transforms and perhaps less than a thousand people in the world knew how to calculate them on a computer. Maybe it was a quirk of fate or maybe it was a cosmic joke, but the free world was depending on me to write code to digitize and process SIGINT into Fourier Transformed signals on a newly purchased CDC 1604 computer.

Jean-Baptiste Joseph Fourier (1768–1830) was a famous mathematician and contemporary of Galois. And like Galois, he was active in the French revolution, earning revolutionary credentials doing time in prison. But he fared better than Galois. For example, he later became the science officer of Napoleon Bonaparte's Egyptian expedition in 1798, and was appointed to a number of important government posts throughout his adult life. But his greatest intellectual achievement was following up on a hunch by Swiss mathematician Daniel Bernoulli (1700–1782) who discovered that all signals are decomposable into oscillating functions like sine and cosine. Whether the signal oscillates or not, it contains perhaps hundreds of oscillating sub-signals with different frequencies—some large, some medium, and many other small frequencies. This was a revolutionary idea then and in 1967. See Figure 4.1.

Even signals that appear to contain absolutely no oscillating waves may be decomposed into oscillating waves! As more waves of the appropriate amplitude and frequency are combined, the sum approximates the non-oscillating signal with greater accuracy. This is the genius of Bernoulli and Fourier—time domain signals are sums of frequency domain signals!

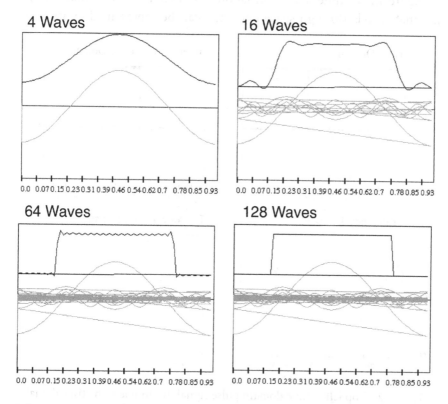

FIGURE 4.1 Fourier's theorem says every (well-behaved) time domain signal is composed of many oscillating frequency domain signals or waves. The approximation to the time domain signal improves as higher frequency waves are added.

(Time domain means the signal varies in time; frequency domain means the signal contains oscillations that differ in frequency.)

To hammer home this incredibly important idea, consider a rather plain pulse signal with apparently no oscillating components, whatsoever, plotted versus time in the top portion of Figure 4.2. The bottom graphs show that the pulse does contain oscillating sub-signals that add up to the flat signal at the top. The bottom left plot is the same information expressed in terms of waves oscillating with different frequencies. The bottom right plot is the same information expressed in terms of the power of each oscillating frequency. Power is important to detecting and decoding the signal because humans respond to the power of a signal more than its time or frequency domain. This is true for machines as well—change in frequency matters as much as change over time, and the power at each frequency is a measure of information content. This is ideal for encoding bits.

Figure 4.2 separates out information in several different formats. A signal that travels through space and time can be represented by its time

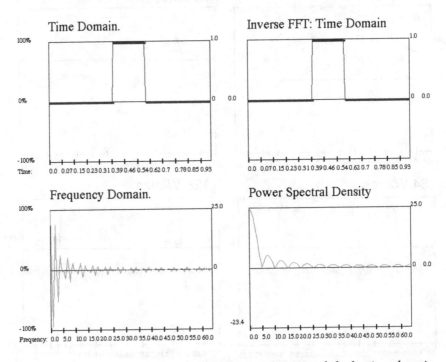

FIGURE 4.2   Top left: a time domain pulse signal. Bottom left: the time domain signal transformed into the frequency domain. Top right: the frequency domain signal inversely transformed back into the time domain. Bottom right: the power spectral density of the frequency domain signal.

domain plot or graph as shown in the upper left of Figure 4.2. It can also be represented by its frequency domain plot or graph as shown in the lower left of Figure 4.2. The plot in the lower right portion of Figure 4.2 graphs power versus frequency, which is important when a human or machines wants to detect and decode the signal. The human ear detects a signal according to the power of its component frequencies.

Gauss's and Bernoulli's profound idea was reduced to a practical method of computation by Fourier and then evolved into an established technique for analyzing time-varying signals by transforming them into a corresponding frequency domain. That is, a signal sent or received as a mathematical function of time is also a collection of oscillating signals, each identified by their frequency. The original signal is recovered from the frequency domain by simply adding up all of its oscillating sub-signals as illustrated in Figure 4.1. Alternatively, the top right signal of Figure 4.2 was obtained from the bottom left frequency domain signal by adding together the waves varying in time with frequency given by the frequency domain graph.

I may have lost the reader, here. What Fourier did was important in two respects. Fourier said:

1. Every well-behaved function of time is composed of the sum of oscillating functions of time, each with a distinct frequency.

2. The Fourier Transform can decompose a function in the time domain into a number of functions in the frequency domain, each with a different oscillation frequency.

3. An inverse Fourier Transform can compose a function in the time domain by transforming frequency domain signals back into a time domain signal.

The Power Spectral Density (PSD) graph of Figure 4.2 represents the distribution of power across oscillating waves or components with different frequencies. Thus, power is distributed across components according to their frequency—not all oscillating waves contain the same amount of power. The lobes of the frequency domain plot of Figure 4.2 are of different amplitudes. This is even more evidence in the power spectral density plot of Figure 4.2, where the amplitude of the lobe represents power. We can pick out individual frequencies by observing the lobes in the frequency domain. Obviously, larger lobes (more powerful components) are of highest interest in terms of carrying information.

The frequency domain obtained by the Fourier Transform reveals the oscillating waves that make up a signal in the time domain. The Power Spectral Density (PSD) graph shows the distribution of signal power across frequencies.

MEANWHILE, 100 YEARS LATER

I had studied most of the great mathematicians of the eighteenth and nineteenth centuries prior to arriving at the giant ball company on Central Expressway in 1967. But, what I did not know was how important Fourier Transforms were to signal processing. I knew even less about how to perform the Fourier Transform on a computer. But that was my job, so I had to learn. In the modern world today, an analog signal such as a blip from radar or a sound wave captured by a microphone or cell phone is digitized and stored or processed by a Digital Signal Processor (DSP). The DSP is a combination of hardware and FFT (Fast Fourier Transform) software that transforms the time domain signal into a frequency domain signal. Normally, the Fourier Transform takes N^2 steps to process N data points. For example, to process 1,024 digitized data points takes over a million steps! Suppose the data points arrive at the rate of 1,024 points per second. The computer must process over a million points per second. This was not possible back in 1967 even though the CDC 1604 was considered a supercomputer.

Infant prodigy Carl Friedrich Gauss (1777–1855) proposed a method that takes only N log N steps to transform N data points. He used it to analyze the periodic motion of the planetary rock Ceres. Over a century after his death, Gauss is still renowned as the greatest mathematician since antiquity. His picture once appeared on the ten-mark bill in Germany, and the Gauss Prize is the highest honor bestowed on mathematicians, today. Like Einstein, Gauss's brain was preserved after his death. His achievements fill many books, but one stands apart from all of the others: the Fast Fourier Transform, or FFT. Gauss used the FFT to reduce the number of arithmetic steps needed to interpolate observations in astronomy.

*The problem is, Gauss published his version of the FFT in neo-classic Latin, which few engineers of the twentieth century understood.**

The importance of saving arithmetic steps may seem absurd when a hand-held smart phone can perform billions of arithmetic operations per

---

* Heideman, M.T., D.H. Johnson, and C.S. Burrus (1984). Gauss and the History of the Fast Fourier Transform. *The ASSP Magazine* Oct. 1984, 1(4).

second, today. But it had profound implications for digital signal processing in 1967, because the FFT made it possible to process N = 1,024 points in only 10,240 steps instead of 1,048,576—an improvement of 100×. By 1967, the Control Data Corporation 1604 minicomputer inside of the building with the giant aluminum ball could handle 10,000 steps per second—but not 1,048,576.* The FFT made the impossible, suddenly possible.

Gauss's method was rediscovered and efficiently implemented on a digital computer by James William Cooley (1926–2016) and John Wilder Tukey (1915–2000) in 1965. Newbie engineers and computer programmers like me feverishly studied the Cooley–Tukey algorithm to discover the delicious secrets of the FFT. The Cooley–Tukey FFT algorithm was eventually implemented hundreds of times by programmers like me to monitor nuclear tests in the Soviet Union and for tracking Soviet submarines. Everyone in the military-industrial complex wanted one of its own. By 1967, Cooley and Tukey were rock stars of the signal processing community.

Eventually, the FFT became a cornerstone of almost all signal processing, and is a crucial component of devices like DVD players, cell phones, and disk drives. It also facilitated the development of common data formats like JPEG, MP3, and DivX used in speech analysis, music synthesis, and image processing. Medical doctors routinely use the FFT for medical imaging, including Magnetic Resonance Imaging (MRI), Magnetic Resonance Spectroscopy (MRS), and Computer Assisted Tomography (CAT scans).

The FFT has been used in other disciplines besides signal processing. It is used to find fast solutions to partial differential equations with periodic boundary conditions, most notably Poisson's equation and the nonlinear Schrodinger equation that describes the motion of quantum particles. Cornell University professor Charles van Loan says, "The FFT is one of the truly great computational developments of this 20th century. It has changed the face of science and engineering so much that it is not an exaggeration to say that life as we know it would be very different without the FFT."[†]

It had to wait for the invention of the digital computer to resurface. And when it did, it changed how we communicate.

---

* CDC 1604 could process about 100,000 operations per second. https://en.wikipedia.org/wiki/CDC_1604
† http://www.cs.princeton.edu/courses/archive/spr05/cos423/lectures/05fft.pdf

A BRIEF INTERMISSION

Why is the Fourier Transform so essential to modern communication? Let me tell another story before jumping into the secrets of the FFT. The Fourier theorem states that any signal transmitted over time like the examples shown here can be converted into oscillating waves with distinct frequencies. In fact, our brain does this when our eyes and ears pick up time-varying signals in everyday life. Our eyes capture light containing colors, which are simply oscillating photon waves at different frequencies. For example, red light is a stream of photons oscillating at approximately 4,835,362,225,806 Hertz. We see the photon vibrations in the time domain but our brain transforms these signals into colors in the frequency domain. White light contains all visible frequencies. The electronic equivalent of white light is called *white noise*, because it contains all frequencies. Humans use white light to see, but machines filter it out in search of signals containing coded information.

The same is true of audio perception. We hear signals buried in noise, but our brain transforms them into tones after filtering out the noise. We see and hear the power contained in each frequency's lobe and interpret the power spectral density as brightness or loudness. Our biological Fourier Transformers are sensitive to orders of magnitude of change, so that a ten-times more intense sight or sound registers as a perceptible step up or down measured in *decibels*. Ten decibels equal a ten-fold change in intensity; 20 decibels equal 100-fold change; and 30 decibels equal 1,000-fold change.

The FFT performs the mathematical equivalent of human eyes and ears by separating a signal into the colors and sounds that make up the signal. Fourier realized that all signals are the sum of waves modeled as sine/cosine functions added together, just like sounds wafting through the air consist of many tones added together. If one tone represents a "1" bit and another tone represents a "0" bit, the FFT can filter out everything except the tones representing "1" and "0." In this way, digital information is transmitted through wires, glass fiber, and the air, captured by a cell phone's antenna, filtered and transformed by an FFT butterfly algorithm, and interpreted as meaningful information.

Fourier made a discovery that would become essential to the operation of smart phones almost 200 years after his discovery, but only became practical after the invention of high-speed computing. In 1967, one of the earliest implementations of this idea as it applied to the modern era of spying was taking place inside of the giant ball off Central Expressway.

Now for the details.

THE DELICIOUS SECRET OF FFT (ADVANCED)

Computationally, the FFT is the sum of sine and cosine functions with different amplitudes and different frequencies. If the computations are done in groups of size 2^n, or powers of two, the algorithm takes advantage of symmetries and redundancies. Essentially, the secret of the FFT is a clever trick. Gordon Sande writes in *Physics Today* that Tukey was,

> Becoming progressively more aware of the redundancy in the arithmetic of Fourier series. [He] communicated his musings to various colleagues. Eventually, a set of notes documenting his notions reached James Cooley by way of Richard Garwin, both of the IBM Thomas J. Watson Research Center. The same content as those notes was also part of Tukey's Mathematics 596 seminar lecture notes in 1963, which were augmented by graduate students. Tukey tried to interest several of his colleagues in pursuing his notions on the redundancy in the arithmetic of the Fourier series. He succeeded twice: One result was the Cooley–Tukey development of the notes communicated through Garwin; the other, the Sande–Tukey development of that part of the Mathematics 596 lecture notes. The two variants are mathematical transposes. The fast Fourier transform was an interesting and useful exercise in clever programming made possible by the unique properties of the complex exponential.*

The clever programming became known as the *butterfly algorithm*, see Figure 4.3. Data flows through the butterfly pipeline from left to right. At each stage, the inputs are multiplied by a weight and combined into a single number. For example, x0 is the sum of weighted inputs s0 and s1. In an interview by Andrew Goldstein in 1997, Cooley explained the butterfly algorithm:

> Dick Garwin said John Tukey was doodling while at one of these meetings, and he asked him what he was doing, and he said well he was working on an idea for doing Fourier transform much faster than people do it now, and it was essentially the idea of taking N, the large number of points, for your transform, writing it as two factors, equal of A × B, and then decomposing the large Fourier transform into sets of small Fourier transform[s] of size A and B,

---

* https://physicstoday.scitation.org/doi/10.1063/1.1397408?journalCode=pto

A and B being the factors of N. And he said to Dick Garwin, if you continue the factorization, you can get a Fourier transform, which does N equal to a power of two, in N log N operations, which was very, very important to Dick Garwin, because at the time they were discussing ways of limiting atomic bomb testing, and Dick Garwin had the idea of setting seismometers all around the Soviet Union, since the Soviet Union wouldn't allow on site testing. So he thought he could do it from outside, but to do it, you would have to process all the seismic signals, and a large part of the processing was, could be done, by Fourier transforms. But the computing power at the time was not enough to process all of the signals you'd need to do this. Now, this was his incentive, but he didn't discuss that, he came to me and he made up another problem. He didn't want to tell me about that.*

Cooley was John von Neumann's computer programmer at Princeton University from 1953 to 1956, and met Tukey when both men worked at

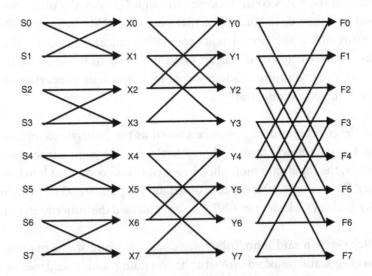

FIGURE 4.3 The butterfly pattern of the FFT is applied to N = 8 data points Log N = 3 times to process N data points in N Log N = 24 steps. At each stage, two numbers are multiplied and summed to obtain a number to be used in the next stage. This pattern repeats with another butterfly pattern spanning twice as many numbers.

---

* http://ethw.org/Oral-History:James_W._Cooley

IBM. Tukey also worked with John von Neumann and coined the term *bit* for binary digit, and is also noted for early use of the term *software* to mean computer instructions and programs that could be changed easily. The FFT was important because it could be used to pick out weak signals from noisy data—a requirement of "trust but verify" in SALT (Strategic Arms Limitation Treaty). It was also the kernel of an idea that I was hired to work on inside the building with the giant ball on top. The FFT was an economical way to sniff out signals called *signatures* from an assortment of SIGINT types. Not only did it work on seismic data, it also worked on audio, visual, and electronic data. It was the key to detecting and cleaning up noisy signals regardless of physical format.

CAN YOU HEAR ME NOW?

The Cooley–Tukey FFT makes it possible for a very weak cell phone signal to be picked out of the air, cleaned up, and made recognizable. It is the fundamental technology for sending and receiving digital information to and from cell phone towers. Figures 4.4 and 4.5 illustrate the effectiveness of the FFT under weak and noisy conditions. As an illustration, suppose the square pulse of Figure 4.2 represents a bit: the pulse is high if the bit equals one and low, otherwise. Sending a bit through a noisy channel presents a challenge to the communications engineer—a challenge met by the FFT butterfly algorithm.

The problem facing the communications engineer is how to separate signal from noise. Figure 4.5 shows how severely the square pulse can be obscured by the addition of random noise such that its information is buried in a random jumble of meaningless data. We cannot determine if the square pulse represents a zero or one unless the noise is removed.

Shannon's theorem says the amount of information that can be transmitted and received depends on the signal-to-noise ratio, S/N. Information is reduced or eliminated altogether if the noise is too high or the signal too low. It is simply drowned out by noise. The FFT plus a filter allows a machine to pick out faint signals by filtering out noise so that a weak signal can be detected and processed even in the presence of noise—up to a point defined by Shannon's theorem. Noise is always present in the background, and as described in previous chapters, the received signal is the sum of information and noise:

$$\text{Received signal} = \text{Information} + \text{Noise}$$

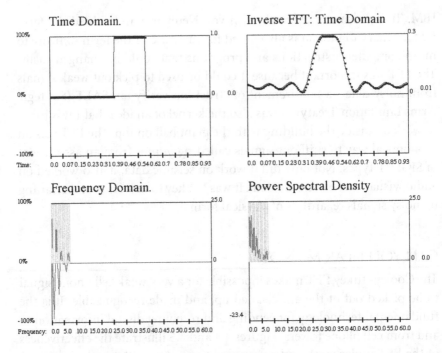

FIGURE 4.4 These graphs illustrate the results of removing frequencies below a certain threshold, and then inversely transforming the frequency domain signal back into the time domain.

The power spectral density of a signal plots signal power versus frequency. Noise is typically a high-frequency perturbation with relative power expressed as the signal-to-noise ratio S/N. Furthermore, S/N appears in the power spectral density plot as low-amplitude, high-frequency lobes. See the bottom plots of Figures 4.4 and 4.5.

If we locate the noise in the frequency domain and filter it out, the noise is removed from the time domain as well. We attempt to keep the more powerful frequencies as revealed by the power spectral density plot, and discard everything else. When the data are transformed back into the time domain, the signal emerges with little or no noise. This is illustrated in Figures 4.4 and 4.5.

Figure 4.4 shows the effects of filtering the pure pulse signal of Figure 4.2. Note that removing its low-amplitude, high-frequency components modifies the time domain signal. Since every signal is a sum of oscillating waves, removal of some waves changes the time domain signal as shown in the inverse FFT time domain of Figure 4.4. However, if we are careful, the general shape of the square pulse survives the round trip

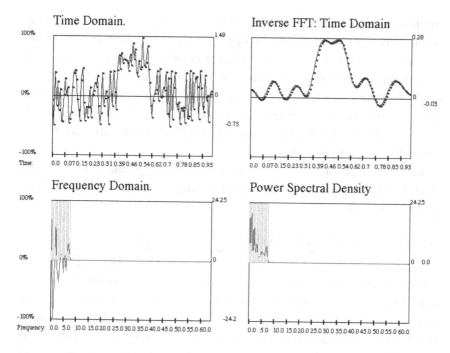

FIGURE 4.5 These graphs illustrate the same technique applied in Figure 4.4 to noisy data as shown in the top left plot. The enhanced data contains less noise, which means it is more accurate. This has its limits, however, but the technique is very effective for amplifying and cleaning weak signals containing sound, images, and messages from spacecraft 13 billion miles away. Filtering essentially enhances the signal-to-noise ratio, S/N, making it possible to transmit more information through noisy channels.

from transform to inverse transform. The inverse FFT signal can still be decoded as a one or zero.

Figure 4.5 shows the effects of filtering the noisy pulse signal of Figure 4.2. A relatively large amount of noise is added to the oscillating sub-signals of Figure 4.2. The same process is repeated as in Figure 4.4: the data are transformed into the frequency domain, the low-amplitude, high-frequency sub-components are eliminated from the power spectral density plot, and the trimmed frequency domain data are inversely transformed back into the time domain. This process removes nearly all noise perturbations.

Being able to transform any signal digitally, as opposed to by analog means is very significant because the digital process is extremely simple. An analog filter requires sophisticated circuits and sophisticated mathematics. A digital filter, on the other hand, requires simple programming. Any filter window can be defined as a function in the frequency domain, or simply as a rule for which frequencies to zero-out in computer memory. The power spectral density and frequency domain data are cleaned up by erasing the unwanted frequencies and transforming back into the time domain as crisper, cleaner data. Nearly one hundred years of elaborate electronic circuit design and fancy filter mathematics is replaced by relatively unsophisticated software.

Digital FFT converts a sophisticated analog filter problem into a trivial digital filter problem solved by software. Simply erase the unwanted frequencies in memory.

SIGNALS ARE MATHEMATICAL FUNCTIONS

It should be clear from the foregoing that electronic signals are formal and rigorous mathematical functions. They are as pure as Newton's Laws of motion—laws that established a rational view of nature. The real world plays by mathematically precise rules. Nonetheless, Newton's laws were eventually overturned for systems operating at very small scales, and at very large scales. Quantum mechanics seems to apply at nanometers and relativity seems to apply at parsecs. Newton's laws fit somewhere in between, but they are not absolute. Where do the mathematical laws of signals fit?

Recognition that signals are mathematical functions leads us to ask, "What else are signals capable of?"

Albert Einstein (1879–1955) had convinced himself of the validity of the theory of relativity by the 1907 Christmas season, and yet it would take him another eight years to clean up the mathematics. He appears to have wandered off task until competition arrived in the form David Hilbert's (1862–1943) sudden interest in relativity theory around 1912, culminating in putting Einstein's radical theory of gravity on firm mathematical grounds in November 1915. The unanticipated competition from Hilbert made Einstein's stomach churn. It also pushed him to clean up his earlier mathematical treatise on gravity, and produce a revised theory that has been validated for nearly a century.

"By June 1911, after a four month stay in Prague, Einstein is again on the general relativity track and on the bending of light. The next important breakthrough comes a year later, in August 1912 when Einstein is back in Zurich and is literally crying for help to his friend and fellow student from ETH: 'Grossmann, you must help me or else I'll go crazy!'"* The mathematics of relativity contributed greatly to his stomach pains. He was stuck.

Hilbert was perhaps the greatest living mathematician during Einstein's life. He is best known for establishing a mathematical object termed "Hilbert space" by one of his assistants, John von Neumann. If there was a mathematical royalty in the early twentieth century, its king was Hilbert. Hilbert space is where the Fourier Transform lives and where it gains foundational status. More importantly, we need Hilbert space to understand what else signals are capable of. While Hilbert had little interest in processing signals, his function space theory provided the missing link between Fourier and the fundamental nature of signals. You might say Fourier and Gauss were hackers, but Hilbert was the true scientist.

A formal and rigorous theory of transforms had been building for perhaps a century when Hilbert turned his attention to what became known as *function spaces*. A function space is an extended Euclidean space where points are functions instead of numbers. A point in Euclidean space is identified by its x, y, and z coordinates, where x is length, y is width, and z is height. We can locate anything in the universe by giving its x, y, and z coordinates relative to some origin, say, the sun.

Note, all three coordinates are needed to pinpoint a location in Euclidean 3-space. Two coordinates are not enough and four coordinates are too many. This condition is known as *orthogonality*. In Euclidean 3-space, directions are orthogonal if they are perpendicular. That is, they do not cast shadows on one another. A set of orthogonal axes form a *basis* for the space if they are orthogonal. All other coordinates can be expressed in terms of these basis coordinates. Furthermore, the dimension of the space is the number of orthogonal basis axes needed to locate a point or function in the space. It takes three basis axes to locate a point in 3-space, and four to locate a point in 4-space.

Instead of points, the elements of the space are functions such as 3sin(x), 2sin(2x), 5sin(3x), etc. Instead of perpendicular axes, the basic sets of functions used to define all transforms in the space are functions such as sin(kx). The projection of a transform onto an axis is called the *inner product*. The inner product of two basis functions is zero because they are perpendicular by definition. They do not cast a shadow on one another. On the other hand, an arbitrary function in function space casts shadows

---

* https://arxiv.org/pdf/physics/0504179.pdf, p. 4.

on one or more basis functions. These shadows are known as frequency amplitudes in the Fourier Transform.

The dimension of the function space is equal to the number of basis functions whose inner product is zero, meaning no basis function casts a shadow on any other basis function. If we compute the inner product (shadows) of all pairs of functions in a function space and the maximum number of mutually perpendicular (orthogonal) basis functions is 3, then the dimension of the space is 3. This is also the minimum number of "coordinates" needed to locate a function in the space.

The dimension of a function space is the number of basis functions needed to define a functional transform—a function of functions.

The Fourier Transform is a function in a Hilbert space defined by orthogonal basis functions. Specifically, the basis functions are sine and cosine functions—waves. The dimension of the Fourier Transform is infinite, because every function (point) can be expressed as the infinite sum of waves. The FFT has finite dimensions, because every function (signal) can be expressed as a finite sum of waves. The FFT is an approximation to the Fourier Transform defined in Hilbert space.

Too heavy? Do not feel bad. Hilbert said this about Einstein, "Every boy in the streets of Gottingen understands more about four-dimensional geometry than Einstein. Yet, … Einstein did the work and not the mathematicians."* Fourier, Gauss, and Cooley–Tukey may not have known about Hilbert spaces, but they were able to do the work of mathematicians. They hacked together the modern theory of signal processing. Hilbert gave them the theory.

Hilbert space is the basis of quantum mechanics, and the concept of a space full of functions instead of simple points has blossomed into more than two dozen spaces with differing definitions of orthogonality (perpendicularity). The FFT transforms a function (signal) into frequencies by projecting or casting a shadow of the time domain signal onto a set of frequency basis functions. It is the lens used to see a function (signal) in terms of its basis functions (waves).

So much for heavy theory, what does this mean in practice?

SPREADING INFORMATION ACROSS THE SPECTRUM

In 1937, Austrian actress Hedwig Eva Maria Kiesler (1914–2000) escaped her husband's autocratic rule to pursue a career in acting. Arriving in

---

* https://arxiv.org/pdf/physics/0504179.pdf, p. 11.

London by way of Paris, she met Louis B. Mayer (1884–1957), the head of the famous MGM movie studio, while he was scouting for talent in Europe. Mayer aimed to create another Greta Garbo or Marlene Dietrich and convinced Hedwig Kiesler to change her name to Hedy Lamarr. She played Delilah opposite of Victor Mature in Cecil B. DeMille's "Samson and Delilah" in 1949.

Hedy was married five times. Her first husband was Friedrich ("Fritz") Mandl (1900–1977), chairman of Hirtenberger Patronenfabrik, a big Austrian weapons manufacturer. The company supplied armaments to Austrian and Italian Fascist governments leading up to and including WWII. Between 1933 and 1937, Hedy attended business meetings with Fritz and absorbed much of the technical discussions. This background may explain why she became interested in the war effort after immigrating to the United States to become a movie star. It also explains how she obtained a technical education.

Lamarr was a compulsive inventor. Her improvements to traffic stoplights and carbonated drinks failed, but she continued to tinker in her spare time between acting jobs. Howard Hughes (1905–1976) lent her the assistance of Hughes Aircraft Company engineers, who he said would, "make anything she asked for."* But her collaboration with composer and pianist George Antheil (1900–1959) proved the most fruitful as it became the basis of modern telephony. The two met when she sought advice on how to enhance her upper torso.† Their conversation eventually turned to the war effort and the problem of preventing radio-controlled torpedoes fired from Allied submarines from being jammed.

Radio-controlled torpedoes could easily be jammed by interfering with the guidance signal, because it was transmitted at a fixed frequency. Once the frequency was discovered, a louder jamming signal could drown out the control signal, veering the torpedo off course. The Lamarr–Antheil idea was simple, but difficult to implement in 1940s technology. To fend off jamming, the two inventors proposed to simply encode the control information in a signal that jumped from one frequency to another. Even better: Randomly jump or hop from frequency to frequency. The jamming signal is rendered ineffective, they reasoned, because the jammer did not know which frequency to jam next.

---

* https://en.wikipedia.org/wiki/Hedy_Lamarr
† https://en.wikipedia.org/wiki/George_Antheil

The Antheil-Markey (her married name at the time) method of frequency hopping was patented in 1942, but not implemented until 1962, during the Cuban Missile Crisis. Because there were few computers and even fewer people with access to digital computers during WWII, and because Antheil understood how a piano worked, the patent describes a frequency coordination mechanism made from paper player-piano rolls. The technical community overlooked it for another 20 years, but the two inventors were eventually recognized and given an award in 1997.

Long after the patent expired, frequency hopping and a related technology known as *spread-spectrum* became standard practice in Bluetooth and Wi-Fi communications. Frequency hopping is called *spread-spectrum*, today.

Spread-spectrum fully exploits the Hilbert space of electromagnetic frequencies by fully exploiting the basis functions underlying every signal. Here is how: Chopping up a signal into segments and shifting each segment from one frequency to another essentially widens the frequency domain to make room for a variety of frequencies. In fact, if enough frequencies are available and selected randomly, they appear as noise. That is, noise and frequency hopping become indistinguishable. Not only does adding what appears to be noise to the shifting signal make it difficult to jam, it spreads the information across more channels, thus increasing the capacity of the transmission. In technical jargon, the information is spread across more spectrum in the frequency domain, which improves capacity and security at the same time.

Spread-spectrum communication deliberately spreads a signal across a wider frequency domain, resulting in a signal with a wider bandwidth.

A pseudo-random number generator is used to add pseudo-noise to the signal and at the same time broaden the frequency domain or bandwidth. As more frequencies and noise are added, the receiver must become better at filtering out the noise and detecting frequencies. Also, as the signal in time gets shorter, the frequency band gets wider. See Figure 4.6. Thus, noise and short pulses broaden the spectrum so that more information can be inserted into the wider band.

ORTHOGONALITY TO THE RESCUE

Figure 4.6 should stimulate the little gray cells of the imagination because it suggests that the frequency domain empties as time domain signals take less time (become shorter pulses). This is how the word "broad" gets into "broadband"—as the time domain signal gets shorter, the frequency

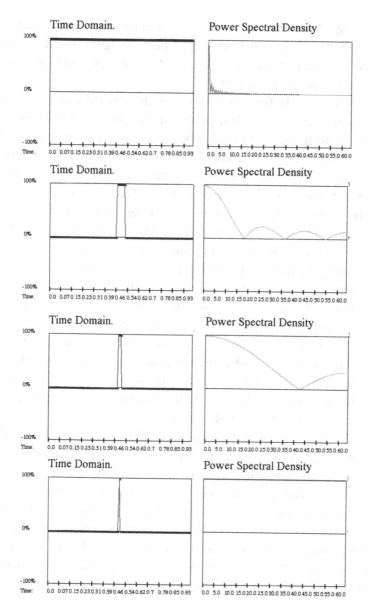

FIGURE 4.6 As the time domain signal on the left becomes shorter, the frequency domain spreads out, as shown in the PSD on the right. This shows how signal power spreads across more frequencies when pulses are shorter, making more room for multiple frequencies. This is the basis of spread-spectrum communications.

domain signal gets broader, eventually flattening out as illustrated in the lower picture of Figure 4.6. Keep this property of signals and their Fourier Transform in mind because spreading like this will explain how quantum signals work too. See Chapter 9.

Why not fill up the frequency domain with more channels so that more time domain signals can be transmitted at the same time? In other words, working in the transformed frequency domain opens up space for sending and receiving more information in the time domain by clever multiplexing. Through careful placement and segmenting of the frequency domain into separate channels, we can send multiple channels of information over perhaps thousands of channels at the same time. This is the idea of OFDM (Orthogonal Frequency-Division Multiplexing), which is the basis of Wi-Fi, Bluetooth, 5G, and most modern communication technologies, today.

Separating the frequency domain spectrum into channels is not a new idea. Thomas Edison and his competitor Elisha Gray had this idea over 100 years ago.* However, they lacked the high-speed, low-cost digital FFT technology that every smart phone contains, today. The idea was far ahead of contemporary technology. Edison and Gray also lacked the mathematical knowledge of the FFT and the underlying concept of orthogonal channels. Hilbert space orthogonality guarantees no crosstalk among the channels. Signals are mathematical functions that we can exploit to cram more information in bands of the spectrum.

In OFDM, a signal is modulated across thousands of frequency channels in the frequency domain, inverted by the inverse FFT, transmitted and received in the time domain. The recipient converts the time domain signal back into the frequency domain via the forward FFT to reveal the thousands of frequency channels containing frequency-encoded information. This requires very accurate frequency tuners at both ends of the transmission. Bluetooth, for example, uses 79 channels, and Wi-Fi uses 14 (2.4 GHz) and an additional 24 channels in 5 GHz Wi-Fi. Upward of 4,096 channels have been used in ultra-wideband applications. OFDM brings us to today.

IEEE 802.11 WI-FI™

Everyone with a smart phone or wireless router at home knows what Wi-Fi is. It is how you connect to the Internet. But, how does Wi-Fi make the connection? Wi-Fi is a radio transmitter and receiver built into a single device that communicates wirelessly among digital devices using a sophisticated modulation/demodulation algorithm based on AM radio. The idea is

---

* https://ieeexplore.ieee.org/stamp/stamp.jsp?tp=&arnumber=5307460

simple, but brilliant. Instead of one carrier and one method of modulating information, Wi-Fi uses QAM (Quadrature Amplitude Modulation). This is a mathematically rigorous name for a simple idea—use many carrier waves instead of one, offset by phase shifts such as 30, 45, and 90 degrees. Recall that carrier waves are simply mathematical functions in Hilbert space, typically cosine functions.

For example, two carrier waves might interfere with one another if not offset by 90 degrees. This is known as *phase-shift keying*, as opposed to *amplitude-shift keying*. Phase-shift keying is essentially an exploitation of orthogonal carrier waves. The carrier waves are of the same frequency, but simply offset in phase-space. These constellations are designated by the number of carrier waves—64-QAM, 256-QAM, etc. For example, 256-QAM is often used in digital cable TV. Arbitrarily high efficiencies can be achieved this way, limited only by noise level and stability of the electronics.

Wi-Fi has a long history entwined with the development of the Internet and other forms of wireless communications. It is the culmination of a long series of inventions and innovations that extended radio into computing, and then into global communication networks we now call the Internet. At the same time that commercial radio was declining because of the adoption of television and the wired Internet, radio communication was becoming increasingly pervasive in hi-tech circles. It would eventually break out and overwhelm other forms of communication, but in the early days, the chain reaction was barely perceptible.

COMMENT

Over the past 150 years, the signal has evolved from a single-stream of time domain dots and dashes of the telegraph to mathematical functions defined as multi-stream orthogonal waves in the frequency domain of Wi-Fi, Bluetooth, and fiber optical cable. Electronic devices routinely calculate Fourier Transforms millions of times faster than Gauss and Bernoulli ever dreamed possible. Clever engineers exploit the fundamental properties of mathematically rigorous function spaces to pack enormous amounts of information in wide swaths of spectrum even as they defeat noise by FFT filtering.

Whether we like it or not, we live in a Hilbert space defining basis functions that are the foundation of Orthogonal Frequency-Division Multiplexing (OFDM). It is such a sound idea that every form of modern communication is converging on QAM.

CHAPTER 5

The Fountainhead

THE WINTER OF 1968–69 was perhaps the coldest on record in Palouse Country. The large thermometer on the Savings and Loan Bank building in downtown Pullman, Washington was stuck at 49 *below zero*. Six-feet-high piles of snow reached for the eaves of my poorly insulated duplex in Fairway student housing, glued to the ground by icicles three feet long. Fortunately, the Computer Center was only a few hundred yards away, and someone had burrowed a trench through the snow to the front door. With coat pulled over my head I sprinted from my building to the Computer Center building, nearly knocking over another Eskimo headed in the opposite direction.

I thought preliminary exams might end my career as a Ph.D. student in Computer Science, but as I ran through the bitter wind and snow to the warm and inviting glass door and then into the nearest heated room, I changed my mind: I was probably going to die from exposure to the elements. My mind drifted—searching for a viable dissertation topic is a waste of time if I am going to perish, anyhow, I thought. Huffing and puffing warm air into my cupped hands, I made my way to the electronics lab where a band of professors were waiting to thin the graduate student herd. I was sucked into the slaughter mostly by the prospect of thawing out than finding a thesis topic.

The meeting had just begun. A professor stood before an Interdata™ Model 8/32 micro-programmable minicomputer as he pitched the IMP to eager upturned faces. He waved a REFERENCE MANUAL with PROPRIETARY INFORMATION stamped across the cover as he explained that the next big push in computer science was going to be linking machines together so they could talk to one another regardless of location, brand, or communication protocols. The US Army had a lot of money to hand out to university researchers, which meant that what he was talking about would become a reality. Yes, there was support for graduate students. No, the projects were not yet defined. Yes, you must write a proposal. Someone blurted out, "What is an IMP?"

"IMP stands for *Interface Message Processor*," explained the professor. "See this Interdata minicomputer behind me?" Everyone looked through him to gaze at the brand new minicomputer painted Ocean Blue. "We are going to turn this machine into an IMP by changing its micro-programming. With a new instruction set it will become an IMP." We all looked at each other.

Best of all, I thought, "I'll get paid."

THE CHAIN REACTION

Nobody knew what the Internet was in 1968. It didn't even have a name. The idea of connecting computers together in one global network was not new, however, as the telegraph system and public telephone system already did that. So what was the big deal about the IMP and the switches and routers that would evolve from them? The professor who briefed the handful of graduate students during that freezing snow and ice storm in the middle of the wheat fields of the Palouse didn't exactly know either. As it turned out, telephone and telegraph technologies were precisely the wrong technologies for the coming Internet age. But at the time, only a few people knew this.

For one thing, telegraphs and telephones are point-to-point, like a telegram or telephone call. For another thing, they are circuit-switched, which means the entire circuit between caller and callee is dedicated to a single conversation at a time. AT&T tied up all of the circuits between my mother and me when I called home at Christmas. Conference calling with two or three people was difficult and expensive because even more circuits would have to be tied up throughout the conversation.

The public telephone system was designed for three-minute calls. Even so, AT&T engineers knew that most of the air time during a telephone call was filled with nothing. The space between spoken words was wasted. The pause between speakers was even more wasteful. Circuit-switched networks, as they were called, were tremendously wasteful. And a telephone call was expensive.

To add insult to injury, the technology for connecting a computer to the telephone was largely proprietary. An IBM computer could not talk to a CDC computer without a lot of expensive equipment in between. Brand X did not cooperate with Brand Y. While this was good for the computer manufacturers, it was not good for consumers, because it locked them into a proprietary system. IBM in particular liked this, because it could sell proprietary software on top of its hardware.

There was not much motivation for IBM to make it easy to connect its competitor's machines together with theirs. Nor was there much motivation for AT&T to allow computer communications on its voice network, because the telephone network was designed to support analog voices and not digital bits. Even worse, AT&T viewed its telephone network as private property—consumers only rented time on a closed system rather than owning time on an open communication system. The legal system supported AT&T. FCC Tariff No. 132 made it unlawful for telephone subscribers to connect their own equipment to AT&T's telephone network. AT&T especially did not like subscribers connecting computers to their network. In fact, AT&T sued people that tried.

Then Thomas Carter came along and changed everything. He invented a small *acoustic coupler* that connected one end to a computer (or whatever you wanted) and the handset of a telephone to the other end. The Carterfone acoustic coupler converted bits into sounds and sounds into bits. The device was slow, but brilliant, because it hacked the AT&T monopoly. The only problem was AT&T didn't like it. According to the telephone company, "No equipment, apparatus, circuit or device not furnished by the telephone company shall be connected with the facilities furnished by the telephone company." AT&T made the mistake of thinking the law backed up their monopoly.

Nicholas Johnson writes,

> Tom Carter's challenge involved the question of how to place and receive phone calls while riding his horse or otherwise getting about on his cattle ranch when the phone was back in the ranch house. He started working on that challenge in 1949 but found the answers much easier with transistors than with vacuum tubes when he returned to the abandoned project in 1958 and promptly produced the first Carterfones. They were essentially acoustic coupling devices that enabled the connection of a telephone handset to a radio transceiver, not that different from those early 300

baud acoustic cup computer modem devices used in the late 1970s and early 1980s. Ultimately some 3,500 Carterfones were sold. As he put it, "we just showed up at oil company shows and started selling … I just didn't believe anyone I wasn't harming had the right to tell me I couldn't be in business." As it turned out, he was correct in believing that AT&T did not have the right to tell Carter he couldn't be in business, but he was wrong if he did not recognize that AT&T did have the motive and means to fight his being in business. By the time of [the] 1968 decision in Carterfone, 100 of his former employees had left the business. Carter, now alone, had to sell his remaining ranch and home. As he said, he "got a lot of moral support but not a dime of financial help." Ultimately he and his wife, Helen, moved to a town with the wonderfully Texan name of Gun Barrel City. In 1984 he said, "[I]t's been a great relief moving down here. We were beat, tired out. I think it has added 10 years to my life." Seven years later, he died.*

Carter sued AT&T for violation of the Sherman Anti-Trust Act, and after a lengthy battle prevailed in 1968. His victory ignited a chain reaction that spelled the end of AT&T's monopoly on communication and started the global movement toward open and free signals. The Carterfone decision opened the floodgates to innovation in communications. It made the idea of an IMP thinkable.

But, someone had to fund the movement.

HEAVY FUNDING

None of the technologies described in this book would have emerged so quickly out of post-WWII science without heavy funding from the US Government. And the fountainhead of government-sponsored R&D was the Information Processing Techniques Office (IPTO) at ARPA (Advanced Research Projects Agency of the Army), and later on, DARPA (Defense Advanced Research Projects Agency). It brought us the Internet, GPS, driverless cars, microprocessors, and robotics, among other things. Later on, NASA and the US Space Program accelerated many of the projects initially sponsored by ARPA, but the visionary ARPA program managers

---

* Johnson, Nicholas (2008). Carterfone: My Story. *Santa Clara High Technology Law Journal,* 25(677). http://digitalcommons.law.scu.edu/chtlj/vol25/iss3/5

were the sparks that ignited the information revolution that began right after WWII. It was the fountainhead.

The story of ARPA and the rise of the Internet have become part of the mythology and reality of the Internet. In fact, it was an unusual outlier agency that defied the stereotype of most government agencies led by bureaucrats and political appointees. It was a one-off. The co-inventor of packet switched signals, Paul Baran (1926–2011) explained this unusual government agency and how it brought us the Internet in a 1988 interview:

> ARPA was very unusual in that it accounted for about 60%, if I recall correctly, of all the computer research in the country, including IBM. So, if you took all the computer research going on, ARPA's budget accounted for about 60% of it. This was in the early '60s, after it was created, and so it was a base of tremendous power, and they were funding research in all the universities, and they sort of had a club. Major universities were members of the club and they would receive their funding faithful and, originally, in fact, the first director of computer research was Dr. J. C. R. Licklider, who was a very competent researcher himself. ARPA was a little different than other government agencies in that it was managed by "honest to goodness" scientists themselves. So you had people who were able to distinguish bullshit from real work, and they had a lot of money and were very flexible in what they allowed people to do. And the secret in funding good research is that you don't get preoccupied with the crap and you look the other way when people spend the money, in ways you think unwisely, and eventually something good comes out of it and you focus on that. So ARPA was funding all the research—not all but a significant piece of it. … ARPA was the *fountain* for all the bucks.*

ARPA/IPTO was incredibly important and successful because of its innovative leaders. Larry Roberts succeeded Robert Taylor and J. C. R. Licklider as director of IPTO—the agency that soon became the hub of the club that Baran describes, in the previous quote. You might say that Roberts was the head in fountainhead. He managed funds, but also made many technological contributions to the projects he funded. For example, he worked out the slotted AlohaNet protocol described, later.

---

* http://archive.computerhistory.org/resources/access/text/2017/09/102740210-05-01-acc.pdf

Roberts and others recognized the limits and boundaries placed on them by AT&T and the big "three-letter" computer companies that dominated communications and computing at the time. But, he was in charge of military computing research, which gave him license to ignore the limits and boundaries of commercial computing. Roberts noticed that the cost of computing was declining much faster than the cost of communications. And what good is a computed result if it cannot be communicated? He also realized that combining computers and communications technologies meant removing the barriers separating two divergent communities—computing and communicating.

Of course there was a third road between computers dominated by IBM and communications systems dominated by AT&T. The telegraph established the first global communications network in the 1840s and 1850s. It even had roots in semaphore technology of the 1790s. Like the Internet nearly a century later, the telegraph industry was the center of nineteenth- and early twentieth-century explosive growth of technology. Binary semaphore signals were organized and standardized by Samuel Morse (1791–1872) and Alfred Vail (1807–1859) and turned into an early protocol for machines called Morse code. They were the Steve Jobs and Steve Wozniak of the nineteenth-century communications revolution.

Morse code is binary. Pressing the telegraph key represents a "1" and not pressing it represents a "0." Morse code evolved and changed along with technology used to communicate information by coding it as sequences of bits. Frenchman Jean-Maurice-Émile Baudot (1845–1903) invented time-division multiplexing for telegraphy and the 5-bit Baudot code, improving on Morse code and the efficiency of transmission lines. The Baudot code would eventually be supplanted by an even more elaborate binary code extended to control machinery like printers and typewriters.

The telegraph's teletypewriter keyboard and printer served as the human interface for most computers in the 1940s and 1950s. More specifically, the ASR-33 teletypewriter was appropriated to handle input and output to computers—something the ASR-33 was never designed to do. However, it worked very well, because of its digital heritage (versus the analog telephone equipment). The workhorse ASR-33 would soon disappear as the computer industry matured, but its influence remains today in the form of descendants of Morse code. ASCII (American Standard Code for Information Interchange) evolved into today's Universal code, but it still contains codes that go all the way back to Morse and Baudot.

So, by the time ARPA came onto the scene, communications between a single teletypewriter machine and a single computer was an established fact. Teletype machines were routinely transmitting and receiving digital information from around the world. They connected machines to one another in what can be considered a very primitive Internet. So, what was the big deal with the IMP? Larry Roberts realized that point-to-point communication between user A and user B was inadequate to the task of linking together many computers from around the world. But a few major obstacles remained in the way of his vision.

It was during Robert's watch that the collection of technologies that eventually became the Internet were cobbled together and demonstrated. The breakthrough came when he read Paul Baran's 1964 article on packets. He said, "All of us in computing were clearly not going to go after it on a circuit switched basis. We were all thinking in blocks in some text." Baran's packets were ideal for Robert's blocks. Packets did not clog up an entire circuit for the duration of the conversation, and a network of interconnected IMPs provided redundant paths through a jungle of unreliable connections. The combination of network redundancy and packet switching appeared to overcome the limits and barriers of telegraph-type systems, and bypassed the tariff-laden public telephone system. This line of reasoning turned out to be disruptive.

Baran assumed any communication network fit for battle must contain unreliable parts by definition. Connections can be damaged, command posts blown apart, and wires brought down. So the concept of a reliable link had to be replaced by something else. Rather than establish a point-to-point connection as in a telephone call between two people, or point-to-point telegraph, why not provide an entire network of connections and let the information flow through the most available paths in the multi-path network? Any network becomes too brittle if each node in the network takes on too much responsibility, he reasoned. Instead, information should be broken into blocks and allowed to weave its way through an unreliable network. Baran called this a *distributed adaptive message block system*—a terminology that was quickly discarded and forgotten.

"So, ideally we would have packets, fixed length, and have some way of detecting whether you had an error or not—a CRC [Cyclic Redundancy Check]. You had a flag that indicated, that you had an indication of who it went to and whom it came from, and at that time it was easier to keep them the same length, because the original design was to do all this in hardware."* Roberts fancied the idea, but the name was too long. Fortunately, distributed adaptive message blocks became known as *packets*.

At nearly the same time, and working separately from the Americans, British scientist Donald Davies (1924–2000) also promoted the idea of packets—breaking up streams of bits into chunks or packets to increase their survivability due to noise or accidental disruptions. Davies called them *packets*—a nomenclature that stuck. Roberts and Davies would eventually meet, but Davies had less influence on the fountainhead than Baran, perhaps because he was located in England and not the United States.

Baran turned out to be right about an unexpected turn of events. The prevailing idea of a computer network back in the 1960s and 1970s was for high-speed computers to consume most of the capacity of the network on their own. People typing away at teletype terminals were slow and computers were fast. So the fast computers are likely to clog up the network. Humans were bottlenecks, not computers. But as it turned out, the bottleneck was the fast computers! The people and network sat idle while host computers were busy doing input and output operations on packets of data! The fast computers were the bottleneck. It soon became obvious that the job of communicating would have to be off-loaded to special computers called IMPs (Interface Message Processors) and TIPs (Terminal Message Processors).

When ARPANet users and developers realized that packet switching should be off-loaded to smaller machines, the logical choice of hardware device was the newly created minicomputers of the late 1960s and early 1970s. They were perfect for handling packet processing. The details were going to be worked out by graduate students looking for thesis topics like I was in 1968. Ultimately, TIP/IMP machines evolved into switches and routers in modern Internet networks. Routers are simply special-purpose computers for directing the flow of packets. And, they are busier than the computers they connect together.

The concept of an IMP became clear by 1970, but it was still not clear what they actually did. An IMP handled packets, but what did "handling packets" really mean? Baran's idea of a loosely connected network of IMPs managing packets as they traveled through multiple paths overcame many limitations of circuit-switched analog communications, but it introduced

---

* Pelkey, James L. (1988). Interview of Paul Baran. Jan 12, 1988. http://archive.computerhistory.org/resources/access/text/2017/09/102740210-05-01-acc.pdf

additional complexity. For example, how does the equivalent of a conference call among many computers and users get sorted out on a packet switched network? Fortunately, Roberts knew someone who had a solution to the *multiple access and collision problem* created by IMPs and packets.

SAY ALOHA

Imagine you are on an island in the middle of the Pacific Ocean and you want to communicate with others located thousands of miles away. Further imagine that telephone calls are limited and expensive because undersea cables are limited and expensive. Add one more thing: you are a young professor at the University of Hawaii looking to make a name for yourself. This is the situation Norm Abramson (1932–) found himself in after graduating from several prestigious universities on the mainland. He decided to take a big gamble and leave the prestigious mainland university life and relocate to the Big Island thousands of miles from action on the mainland. He rationalized that living on an isolated island in the middle of the Pacific was an opportunity, not an obstacle.

Abramson's idea was audacious for 1970. He proposed building an island-wide radio packet network for connecting people and computers together using satellites! People from isolated islands in the archipelago could login to a large mainframe computer located at the University of Hawaii in what we call "cloud computing," today. Teletypewriters need not be in the same room as the mainframe. Instead, they would tap into a network of IMPs that in turn tap into a radio network hosted by satellites passing by overhead. The AlohaNet was the first wireless Internet.

Abramson had the right idea, but no money. Only someone like Larry Roberts and a deep-pocketed agency like the fountainhead could appreciate his big idea. According to an interview conducted by Severo Ornstein in 1990, Abramson headed off to Washington, D.C. to meet with Larry Roberts, explaining:

> Sometime in 1972, I was visiting [Larry] Roberts' office in Washington for discussions dealing with both technical and administrative matters in the ALOHA system when he was called out of his office for a few minutes to handle a minor emergency. While waiting for Roberts' return, I noticed on the blackboard in his office a list of the locations where ARPA was planning to install IMP's [Interface Message Processors—the first Internet routers] during the next six month period together with the installation

dates. Since I planned to bring up the question of installation of an IMP at the ALOHA system laboratory in Hawaii to be used with the satellite channel discussed above, I took the chalk and inserted 'the ALOHA system' in his list and beside it placed the date of December 17 (chosen more or less at random). After Roberts' return we continued our discussion but, because of the rather long agenda we did not discuss the installation of an IMP in Hawaii, and I forgot that I had inserted an installation date of December 17 for us in the ARPA schedule on his blackboard. … About two weeks before the December 17 date, we received a phone call from the group charged with the responsibility of installing the IMP's asking us to prepare a place for the equipment. On December 17, 1972, an IMP connecting the ALOHA system to the ARPANET by means of the first satellite channel in the network was delivered and installed.*

The AlohaNet was both simple and complicated. It was simple, because it used existing technology such as a teletypewriter at each land-based site called a *node*, and a central computer at the University of Hawaii. Packets contained 80 characters just like the punched cards of an IBM system circa 1965. Signals were based on everyday ham radio operator frequencies communicating with existing satellites. The IBM system was capable of time-sharing multiple users at the same time, and it was much faster than humans typing at a teletypewriter. What could be simpler?

It turned out to be more complicated than it appeared, because of messy details like the fact that everyone would use the same frequency or radio waves at the same time. Even though the information would be packaged into packets and packet switched, there needed to be some mechanism for all nodes to communicate on the same frequency and talk at the same time. Data sent from a teletypewriter flowed at a snail's pace of only 80 characters per second, but when two stations tried to talk at the same time, both transmissions got garbled. Then data had to be manually sent again. It was a pain in the posterior.

Aloha never solved this problem, but it sparked interest in others, most significantly Robert Metcalfe, who had recently arrived from the mainland to find out what Aloha was all about. Metcalfe, like thousands

---

* Abramson, Norman (1985). Development of the ALOHANET. *IEEE Transaction on Information Theory*, IT-31(2), pp. 119–123. http://web.mit.edu/modiano/www/6.263/Abramson_41.pdf

of other graduate students in search of a thesis topic, was very interested in packet switching and resolving the multiple access and collision problem. And, he knew the right people at the right time—Robert Taylor of ARPA and then Xerox PARC.

Robert Taylor had left ARPA and taken a position at the newly formed Xerox PARC located at ground zero in Silicon Valley. He offered Metcalfe a job even after Metcalfe informed him he had flunked his Harvard Ph.D.! The topic of his dissertation was ARPANet related, so it made sense for Taylor to take a chance on the young student. He advised Metcalfe to relocate to the West Coast and work on his dissertation, later.

Metcalfe often crashed at Internet pioneer Steve Crocker's house,

> Steve had a couch in his living room - an important couch. During one visit in 1972, I opened it and got ready to go to sleep, but I was jet-lagged. I'm thrashing about for something to read. He had some shelves. I stumbled across a book called *AFIPS Conference Proceedings* ... not, you might safely say, your typical bedtime reading ... [it] contained a paper about a radio-based network of computers called AlohaNet, developed at the University of Hawaii. As I'm reading it, not only do I understand it, but I disagree with it.*

Metcalfe ran straight into the multiple access and collision problem that eventually became the central contribution of his Harvard Ph.D. dissertation, which he eventually completed. Manually retransmitting 80 characters following a collision just wouldn't do. Carrier Sense Multiple Access with Collision Detection (CSMA/CD) simply had to be automated. It had to become an integral part of the protocol for two or more machines competing for air time. CSMA/CD evolved into a protocol that became known as Ethernet. And Ethernet eventually became part of the TCP/IP algorithm that defines the Internet.

Here is what CSMA/CD does. When a transmitting node detects another signal while transmitting its packet, it stops and transmits a jam signal, waits for a random length of time, and then tries to transmit the packet, again. If a subsequent collision occurs, the node waits even longer before re-trying. In this way, heavily loaded networks reduce congestion

---

* Kirsner, Scott (1998). The Legend of Bob Metcalfe. *Wired*, 11.01.98. https://www.wired.com/1998/11/metcalfe/

rather than contribute to it. All other nodes back off a random length of time when they hear the jam signal. In modern terms, CSMA is part of the MAC (Media Access Control) layer—the lowest layer in the TCP/IP stack, as it is now called.

CSMA/CD was and is a critical technology for making the Internet work whether the signal travels over wires or through the air. It universally solves the multiple access and collision problem not unlike how humans solve the problem when one person interrupts another.

Abramson documents the connection between AlohaNet and Ethernet,

> In his doctoral dissertation, he [Metcalfe] coined the term 'packet broadcasting' to emphasize this distinction. When his dissertation was complete, he spent several months with the ALOHA system, working with Richard Binder who had developed our software and network protocols. Metcalfe then joined the Xerox Palo Alto Research Center, and his development of Ethernet (with David Boggs) at Xerox in Palo Alto demonstrated the effectiveness of packet broadcasting on a cable based medium.*

LET THE SCREAMING AND YELLING BEGIN

Ethernet solved the lower-level problem of colliding packets, but the story doesn't end there. AlohaNet showed the way, but like a compass without a map the road ahead was still uncertain. Even after AlohaNet became operational, a primitive ARPANet consisting of nodes located at 30 institutions and labs operated on different interfaces, packet sizes, labeling conventions, and transmission rates. For example, some packets were 80 characters long, and others were 40. Fortunately, ARPA changed its name to DARPA and kept advancing the technology as well as evangelizing it. Most important, DARPA continued to be the fountainhead in terms of money and ideas.

The TIPs and IMPs shielded users from some of this lack of standardization, but the network was getting too big to ignore the problem much longer. Robert Kahn (1938–) went to work for Larry Roberts and recruited Vint Cerf from Stanford University to help. Together they developed and formalized a comprehensive protocol for information interchange,

---

* Ibid., Abramson.

which became TCP/IP (Transmission Control Program/Inter-networking Protocol)—the lingua franca of the Internet.

The Cerf–Kahn partnership began in a strange way. They had collaborated earlier on a project that attempted to lock up the Internet! Theoretically, one could request access to a machine that was waiting on your machine, and vice versa, so a "deadly embrace" ensued. A circular wait that never terminates is called a *deadlock*. The question is, "Can the ARPANet deadlock, on purpose or accidentally?" The answer back in 1973 was "yes." Kahn and Cerf were rejoined to re-design and standardize the protocols used by TIPs and IMPs. This time, it had better not lead to deadlock.

In a 1999 interview, Cerf explains how TCP/IP emerged over a period of years,

> It was the group at Stanford that did the initial detailed design of TCP. I mean they did the detailed design where we got down to the specifics of state diagrams and everything else, such as packet formats. We published that in December of '74. Then implementation work began, and we got involved with Bolt Beranek and Newman and University College London to collaborate on the testing of the protocols. So, we started the testing work in 1975, after having completed the first specification. We almost instantly discovered we needed to make changes in the design. We went through several iterations. This takes you up to the point where around 1978, when we standardized on version 4 TCP protocol, which is what you are using today. It took us another five years to complete implementations of the now standardized TCP/IP protocols on about 30 different operating systems. Then required that everyone on January 1, 1983 flip over from the existing ARPANET protocols to the new Internet protocols. There was a lot of screaming and yelling and protests.*

So one formal definition of the Internet and its origin is IP v.4 in 1983, because that is when the first solid version of TCP/IP was released and the screaming and yelling began. It is also when the name "Internet" began to seep into the English language. Internet is short for Inter-network, which some people thought contained too many syllables to pronounce!

---

* https://ethw.org/Oral-History:Vinton_Cerf

What was so significant about TCP/IP? First and foremost, it formalized how to connect fully automatic machines together in a community of hundreds, and eventually thousands of machines without deadlocking them. Secondly, TCP/IP fulfilled Baran's concept of information flowing reliably through an unreliable network. IP avoids collisions just like Ethernet, and TCP re-transmits broken streams of messages. It also routes packets through alternate paths to avoid congestion. And, TCP/IP is simple.

The impact of telegraphy can be seen in the origins of TCP/IP. One computer initiates a connection to a destination computer by sending ASCII/telegraph ACK and SYN control signals to get the destination computer's attention. The destination computer replies with a simple telegraph control signal to synchronize the two computers. Transmission of packets commences after the two are synced.

The impact of IBM's 80-character punched card began to fade with the rise of packets. If a packet is too big, it increases the chance of re-transmission because of an error. If it is too small, it increases the work of IMPs trying to route it through an unreliable network. IP v.4 settled on 256 bits of information per packet—a balance between error rates and re-transmission overhead.

Baran's idea of packets finding their own way through the network is implemented in the Cerf–Kahn protocol by an OSPF (Open Shortest Path First) routing algorithm. Each router (IMP) contains a table of neighboring destination routers. Packets are sent to the router along the shortest path, first, but if it is congested, then the next-shortest path is selected, etc. This means that packets can arrive at their destination out of order. It is TCP's job to sort them out and present the stream of packets in proper order. Packets are re-sent if an error is detected, which may further exacerbate packet order. TCP solves both problems at once.

The commercialization of the Internet has increased the use of economic or business rules for routing packets through the global Internet. More recently, the OSPF rule has been replaced by the Cheapest Route First rule that selects routers and paths through the Internet according to cost. This sometimes leads to surprising routes. For example, to send packets from New York to Chicago, the cheapest route might run through a server in Hong Kong!

TCP/IP became a political topic in 2015–2018 when the net neutrality controversy broke out. Net neutrality means every online content producer and consumer should enjoy the same transmission speeds and access. There should be no discrimination on the part of Internet Service Providers (ISPs), and certainly no throttling of bandwidth. The net neutrality controversy reached political levels when the US Government decided to regulate the Internet. This is likely to have major ramifications for the future of TCP/IP. By the time you read this, TCP/IP may have already been changed to accommodate politicians.

Let the screaming and yelling begin.

ORIGINAL SIN

The openness and simplicity of TCP/IP is also cause for concern in the era of unauthorized hacking and online theft. TCP/IP is inherently non-secure, because it was designed to be open and non-proprietary. There were many proprietary network protocols that competed with TCP/IP in 1978, but they were limited by lack of interoperability. TCP/IP solved the interoperability problem, but created another problem—lack of security.

The original sin of TCP/IP, and the Internet in general, is the fact that nothing in the design of TCP/IP protects consumers from unauthorized use, hacking, and the spread of malicious code. Criminal use of the Internet was never anticipated by the Internet pioneers. Vint Cerf warned of an impending "digital dark age" in a 2015 interview.

> He acknowledges that security wasn't on his mind in the early days of the Internet. When he was developing TCI/IP for the Department of Defense in the early 1970s, he worked through all the possible "failure modes" but not possible attacks, he said at a City Arts & Lectures talk last week in San Francisco. That was partly because he assumed all the links would be encrypted and partly because he "wasn't thinking about global availability in the civilian world." So, encryption and other security was retrofitted in. If I had to do it all over again, he said, he'd put public key into the underlying Internet protocols and would have used 128-bits for Internet addresses instead of 32-bits.*

Why is the Internet inherently unsecure? The 30,000-foot answer lies in biology and the concept of a monoculture. In biology, a monoculture describes an ecological system with very low diversity. All members of

---

* https://www.bateman-group.com/banter/hacking-vint-cerfs-wine-cellar-or-why-we-need-to-secure-the-internet-of-things

the system share the same weakness or susceptibility to a certain disease. An attack on one member is an attack on all members. The Irish potato famine dramatically demonstrates how dangerous it is to rely on a single variant of potato.

The TCP/IP standard and all of the subsequently developed standards for how to communicate, format, transmit, and process information forms a globe-spanning monoculture. An attack on one Internet switch, server, or website is an attack on all, because they have the same DNA. The Internet DNA starts with TCP/IP, and continues to permeate the entire Internet ecosystem through basic protocols like SNMP (Simple Network Management Protocol) for controlling routers and switches to SMTP (Simple Mail Transfer Protocol) for sending and receiving e-mail. Add to this list the culture of openness and decades of ignoring security and you have the formula for unmatched fragility. This situation is unlikely to last.

The future of the packet-switched Internet is change.

COMMENT

The story of the Internet has been told so many times that it is part myth and part truth. I have tried to separate the myth and reality, here, with this re-telling—largely in the words of the pioneers, themselves. The truth is, we do not know the extent of its impact on the future of humanity. The pioneers were big thinkers, even predicting an intergalactic Internet. The average teenager today thinks the Internet has always been with us even as a billion people know nothing of its existence. Reality lies somewhere in between.

The concept of a packet is fundamental as is the concept of multiple access with collision detection and rollback. It seems obvious today, but it was radical at the time. An electronic system should not be as flexible and adaptable as the 1973 ARPANet was. One had to think out of the box to imagine it.

While TCP/IP borrowed from the teletypewriter, it too stepped out of the hardware box most innovators found themselves in during the early years. How might an electronic circuit be able to sort out-of-order packets into proper sequence upon arrival? How long must the recipient wait before asking for re-transmission? If the solution depends on software, how can it be made to run fast on relatively slow hardware? These challenges were met by re-imagining decades of traditional communications system's design. It wasn't easy.

CHAPTER 6

The Day the Music Died

B RUCE AND I STEPPED off the plane in Frankfurt and immediately began looking for a map of Germany to see where the headquarters of Nixdorf Computer Company was located. Founder and CEO Heinz Nixdorf (1925–1986) had offered to send the corporate airplane to pick us up, but we had other plans—to rent a fast car and test it on the autobahn. Nixdorf headquarters was located in Paderborn, a historic city founded by Charlemagne and strategically located at the entrance of the industrial state of North Rhine-Westphalia. By 2018, the North Rhine-Westphalia area was home to a handful of vanishing coalmines. It might be considered the Pittsburgh of Germany. At any rate, back in 1976 we thought the drive was exhilarating as well as scenic.

Nixdorf eventually became part of Siemens-Nixdorf, and then the global conglomerate Siemens AG. Heinz Nixdorf was an admirer of Konrad Zuse (1910–1995), arguably the inventor of the first programmable computer in 1941, along with its high-level programming language, Plankalkul. Zuse built and installed many of the first computers in Germany immediately after WWII. Had Germany won the war, we would most likely be calling von Neumann machines Zuse machines. But, that is the topic of another book.

Bruce and I had planned to spend our summer working for food—giving talks throughout Europe in exchange for travel and per diem. The Nixdorf visit was our maiden voyage. We arrived at the computer-climate-controlled headquarters building, gave our brilliant talks, and then enjoyed seeing what the researchers at Nixdorf were up to. This was midstream in the flow of minicomputers and Nixdorf had some of the best aimed at business. They were especially advanced with respect to combining communications with computers in the office environment.

One project in particular surprised me. It was the first time I had seen a real-world application of information theory. This was 1976, but even then the Nixdorf team asked an interesting question, "How do you compress data so it can be transmitted faster over slow communication lines?" I had not really thought of compression as a technology for transmitting information instead of storing it. But in hindsight, it makes perfect sense.

I explained Huffman codes, and how the Huffman tree algorithm easily compresses data as far as it can be compressed. But the German engineers were not satisfied. "No, no, you do not understand. We don't care if the information is completely preserved. We are willing to sacrifice purity for speed." They were thinking in terms of lossy compression, while I was thinking in terms of lossless compression. What is the difference?

Most signals today, containing information in the form of images, videos, speech, music, etc. are compressed to better use bandwidth and to reduce storage requirements. The Nixdorf engineers were ahead of their peers in terms of understanding the importance of compression to the transmission of the signal—not simply as a means of saving storage space, but as a means of improving transmission. In fact, we owe modern compression technology to the Germans. They invented basic MP3, and somewhat by force of first-mover, established the foundation for all modern forms of lossy signal compression.

And, they killed the music industry—as we knew it before MP3 was invented.

HUFFMAN CODE IS LOSSLESS

Lossless compression squeezes out all redundancy leaving only true information. That is, no information is lost due to removal of bits. Once all redundancy has been removed, the remaining bits are information bits, and the amount of information content is equal to the number of remaining bits. Lossless compression reduces to a simple task of sorting the symbols according to their frequency of occurrence. David A. Huffman (1925–1999) understood the connection between frequency of a symbol and its information content. The more often a symbol appears in a signal, the fewer bits are needed to encode it.

Bruce and I earned extra cash lecturing to career IBM employees camped out each summer on the UC Santa Cruz campus where Huffman led a young computer science department. Between lectures we ate like starving undergraduates in the campus cafeteria and listened to Huffman explain his compression algorithm. Mostly, we talked about mountain climbing and snorkeling in the Pacific Ocean.

Huffman invented the first truly practical compression algorithm based on Shannon's information theory while a graduate student at Ohio State University in 1951. His switching theory instructor, Robert M. Fano (1917–2016)—co-inventor of the Shannon–Fano code—assigned the following unsolved problem to Huffman's class. He had done this many times before, with little success. So Fano must have been surprised when Huffman actually came up with a solution superior to his own Shannon–Fano code.

According to Huffman, "The problem was to reduce to the absolute minimum the average number of questions necessary to identify one message — or document, or other object — out of a set of messages, when those messages might not appear with equal frequency, and when the questions had to be phrased so that they could be answered only with either 'yes' or 'no.' I knew that, if I could solve the problem, I wouldn't have to take the final in the course."*

A completely random file cannot be compressed without loss of information, because uniformly random occurring symbols contain maximum information per symbol. No symbol is redundant relative to all other symbols. A lossless compression algorithm exploits the non-uniformity in the distribution of symbols to reduce the number of bits needed to encode the symbols. Common symbols contain less information so they should require fewer bits. Rare symbols contain more information so they should require more bits. Huffman realized that non-uniformity of occurrence meant there was a way to encode non-uniformly occurring symbols using fewer bits. He solved the problem by working from the bottom up as shown in Figure 6.1.

Figure 6.1 shows the Huffman tree for compressing Benford numbers described in Chapter 2, Table 2.1. It works from the bottom up: combining the least frequent pair of symbols into a node marked with the sum of the two siblings. For example, symbols 8 and 9 are least frequent, so they are combined into a node with a frequency of $(4.6 + 5.1) = 9.7\%$. Similarly, symbols 6 and 7 are combined yielding 12.5%, and 4 and 5 combined yielding 17.6%. At each level of the tree, select the two smallest frequencies and combine them to get a combined node in the next level up in the tree. Eventually, the root of the tree contains 100%, or all of the symbols.

---

* http://www.huffmancoding.com/my-uncle/david-bio

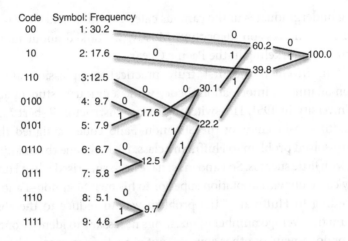

FIGURE 6.1   The Huffman tree of Benford numbers uses 31 bits to encode the nine symbols. The weighted average from Huffman coding is 2.92 bits per symbol. Shannon's equation yields 2.88 bits/symbol, assuming the same frequency distribution, and optimal coding. Shannon's equation yields 3.48 bits/symbol if the distribution of leading digits is assumed to be uniformly random.

Huffman's code is deceptively simple and elegant. Numbering the branches zero or one along a path from root to leaf establishes the code. For example, 00 encodes the "1" symbol using only two bits. Symbols "4" through "9" require four bits. The code for "4," for example, is obtained by tracing the path from the root to the symbol along four links: 0→1→0→0. Note that the least-frequent symbols require more bits, because they contain more information. Information is surprise and infrequent symbols contain more surprise when they actually appear in a signal.

Shannon's formula says Benford numbers contain 2.88 bits of information per symbol. The expected number of bits in Figure 6.1 is 2.92 bits, so Huffman's code isn't perfect, but it comes within 1.3% of optimality. That is, Huffman's code compresses out most of the redundancy, leaving 98.7% "pure information" after compression. A perfect uniformly random distribution of leading digits yields 3.48 bits per symbol according to Shannon's equation. Knowing the non-uniform frequency distribution ahead of time is a form of a priori information that we used to compress the data. The effectiveness of lossless compression depends on how much a priori information is in the data.

Redundant data contains less information. This chapter contains approximately 2.6 megabytes of information, but consumes 4.3 megabytes of data storage, because of redundancy and non-uniformity of symbol frequency. Using a compression algorithm like .ZIP, any non-random file can be reduced in size without loss of information by exploiting redundant or high-frequency patterns, characters, symbols, etc. This is the idea used by the .ZIP compression algorithm.

Phil Katz (1962–2000) created the .ZIP compression algorithm in 1989 using techniques inspired by Huffman trees. Essentially, every compression algorithm minimizes the number of bits needed to encode symbols, but without destroying the way back. Lossless compression techniques can be reversed using tables stored with a compression format such as .ZIP. These tables are used to reverse compression, putting compressed bits back into original and redundant form.

I explained all of this to my German hosts, but they shook their heads in disagreement. I still did not understand their objections until many years later. I described Huffman's lossless compression algorithm while they were already thinking in terms of lossy compression. In lossy compression, some of the information is thrown away—never to be found again. The trick is to know which information to throw away.

TO BE, OR NOT TO BE REDUNDANT

Information is what is left over after all redundant data is removed. But, earlier we added redundancy to the signal to detect and correct errors! Shannon's formulation of information as surprise seems to contradict the concept of error-free signals carrying information, even when there is noise. We added redundancy to secure the signal, and now data compression removes all redundancy! What is wrong with this picture?

In a pristine environment where there is no noise, we can discard the Hamming code, Reed–Solomon code, and all other forms of redundancy, because without noise there are no errors. But in reality, noise always exists in one form or another. Shannon realized this and derived an equation that defines the amount of useful information C we can extract from a noisy channel with bandwidth B, measured in bits per second. If S/N is the signal-to-noise ratio, then C is the maximum information-carrying capacity of a channel such as an Internet connection, Wi-Fi wireless connection, or simply yelling in someone's ear.

$$C = B \log_2 \left(1 + S/N\right)$$

Clearly, if there is no noise, then the S/N ratio is exactly 1.0 and C = B. But, if noise exists, it decreases channel capacity, accordingly. For example, if $S/N = 0$, $C = 0$, and no information is received. The Hamming H(7, 4) code requires 7 bits to carry 4 bits of information, so it is 57% efficient. If H(7, 4) adequately compensates for noise, then S/N is 0.57, and $C = 0.65B$. That is, each H(7, 4) code word reduces channel capacity by approximately one-third.

I felt kind of smug after leaving the Nixdorf building and continued my lecture tour with Bruce. The Germans probably thought I was stupid, because I missed the entire point: how does one compress out the useless information while keeping the useful information intact? I did not understand the difference between Shannon's mathematical formulation of information content, and a human's ability to perceive information.

Take music, for example.

MUSIC TO THE HUMAN EAR

Karlheinz Brandenburg (1954–) studied under psychoacoustic expert Dieter Seitzer at the University of Erlangen-Nuremberg. Seitzer invented a digital jukebox way before its time. His patent application was rejected by the patent office on the grounds that it was impossible. His digital jukebox was a system where people could connect to a central server and order music on demand, over 1980s ISDN digital telephone lines that were beginning to appear across Germany. His "impossible" invention would eventually become not only possible, but hugely successful incarnations like Apple iTunes and Spotify.

In the 1980s, the problem was, digital music files were simply too large to be transmitted, even over ISDN. A typical song might contain 3–5 megabits of data. To send music files over contemporary ISDN lines, Seitzer would need to compress the file down by a factor of almost 12-to-1. He assigned the problem to Brandenburg to work out the details.

With Brandenburg's knack for engineering and Seitzer's deep knowledge of psychoacoustics, the two should be able to build a digital jukebox that worked over ISDN lines with enough fidelity to sound like music to the human ear. That is, they should be able to combine standard electrical engineering with out-of-the-box psychoacoustic engineering to come up with something entirely new. The devil was in the details.

Brandenburg listened to the clear acapella voice of Suzanne Vega (1959–) as she sang "Tom's Diner" for perhaps a thousand times. He could hear the deep lows and also the thin highs as her voice boomed out from a digitized audio track. It was the late 1980s—the height of the analog compact cassette tape player, and a decade before anyone would care about digital audio, because hardware was too expensive. Everyone knew that analog was the only way to maintain quality at a reasonable cost. But Brandenburg and colleagues at the Fraunhofer Institute knew better, because they were willing to settle for imperfect compressed audio as long as it still sounded good.

And one more thing: they were willing to throw away some information in exchange for ten-to-one compression.

The trick was to mask out frequencies that the human ear could not hear anyhow, and enhance the frequencies that humans hear most when a recording is played back. Brandenburg repeatedly listened to playback of "Tim's Diner" until Suzanne Vega's voice sounded just right to his keen sense of sound. If he removed too much, her voice sounded awful. If not enough, the file was longer than it needed to be. In a sense, he needed to simulate how humans hear rather than how machines convert sounds into waveforms and back again. This is where psychoacoustics comes in.

He recalls the process of finding just the Goldilocks balance between discarded information and essential information:

> In 1988 when I thought, "OK, that's near perfect, what we've done," I heard about this song and then heard it myself — it's the acapella version [of Tim's Diner]. The CD is Solitude Standing. The way it's recorded — with Suzanne Vega in the middle and little bit of ambience and no other instruments — is really a worst case for the system as we had it in 1988. Everything else sounded quite OK, and Suzanne Vega's voice was destroyed... Finally [we] perfected the system and then Suzanne Vega's voice was easy, but it gave us quite some work to have her voice in full fidelity ... I think over time I have listened to the song 500 or 1,000 times. In fact, I still like it. That was the good part about it ... Interesting thing, later on I met Suzanne Vega and I heard her singing this song in a live performance. It was really astonishing — [it] was exactly like on the CD.*

Originally designed for transmission over relatively slow ISDN telephone lines, MP3 evolved into the defacto standard for an entire industry and eventually the global Internet. A decade later, Brandenburg and

---

* Rose, Joel and Jacob Ganz. (2011). The MP3: A History of Innovation and Betrayal. https://www.npr.org/sections/therecord/2011/03/23/134622940/the-mp3-a-history-of-innovation-and-betrayal

colleagues settled on the name MP3 because it became the file type used by music-sharing sites like Napster. Even later, the Moving Picture Experts Group (MPEG) adopted it for compressing audio and video into a file small enough to be transferred easily. For example, a song sampled at 128 K bits/second is typically ten times smaller than the uncompressed file. This not only saved storage space but made transmission ten times faster.

MP3 compression uses a technique called *perceptual coding* based on *psychoacoustic models* of how humans perceive sound. Perceptual coding means discarding sounds that are less audible to human hearing. A good pair of ears can hear sounds in the range of 20 to 20 K Hertz, in increments of 2 Hz. Most ears are most sensitive to sounds in the frequency range of 2 K to 5 K Hz. Even within this range, some sounds are not perceived by the human ear because they are overwhelmed by other sounds. In technical terms, some frequencies are masked by other frequencies.

MP3 divides these frequencies into 32 slices and then applies the cosine version of the FFT (Fast Fourier Transform) to each slice before going through a psychoacoustic filter that applies masking—replacing or removing frequencies that cannot be heard by humans. Recall from the previous chapter on FFT, humans respond to frequencies rather than time-varying signals. The FFT simply converts the time domain signal into a frequency domain signal that is compatible with how humans hear. The cosine FFT is considered better than the general FFT because it compacts the signal into fewer frequencies. Fewer is better when it comes to compression.

The FFT process transforms the music signal into 576 frequency bins. Humans cannot hear this well, so Brandenburg took advantage of the opportunity to remove some information and compress the remaining frequencies. His method had to be simple and elegant, and it was! The 576 bins are reduced to 22 bins by simply scaling and rounding off in a process called *quantization*. For example, numbers in the range of 0 to 200 can be squeezed into the range of 0 to 10 by simply dividing by 20 and rounding off the fraction. Frequency 128 becomes 6 and then when converted back into the original range, becomes 120. The compressed signal is more compact, but also has less fidelity. In general, limiting the range of frequencies reduces file size, along with fidelity. Quantization metes out the desired amount of compression by scaling and rounding off the frequency domain signal to any desired level.

After frequencies in the 576 bins are scaled by a factor that reduces them to 22 bands, the remaining frequencies are compressed using the Huffman compression algorithm just described. Recall that Huffman codes compress by assigning a shorter code to more frequent symbols and longer codes to less frequent symbols. Thus, Huffman compression reduces the number of symbols needed to encode redundant information by exploiting the non-uniform probability distribution of symbols. In a given song or voice recording, some frequencies will occur much more often than others. The Huffman algorithm exploits unevenness in likelihood of frequencies. This reduces the number of bits required to store and transmit a frequency.

Huffman coding is lossless, which means we can convert the compressed signal back into its original form. But psychoacoustic filtering destroys this ability, because information is discarded in the masking process. Empirical studies tell us which sounds we cannot hear when overlaid on other sounds. If a sound "drowns out" another sound, MP3 simply removes it, because your ear cannot hear it, anyway.

Frequencies are compressed into two parts using a scale factor and the Huffman code word. Pairs of 576 bins are combined into frames and frames combined into tracks. The process is reversed when a song, for example, is played back from an MP3 compressed file. The frame is decomposed into two granules of 576 bins, the Huffman code word and scale factor applied to each, and the resulting expanded signal converted into an audio signal we hear when the file is processed by a device. Audio uses a PCM (Pulse Coded Modulation) algorithm to digitize audio and the same PCM in reverse to play audio.

MP3 combines old ideas with new to find a balance between information loss and compression level. FFT and Huffman codes are old ideas, while scaling and combining frequencies (masking) are new ideas. The result is something entirely new. In fact, MP3 has been so successful as a combination of theory and practicality that it has been copied many times.

MORE DEVIANT INNOVATION

The MP3 file format won out over other formats such as WAV and AIFF for one simple reason: it enabled music to be stolen. Napster is responsible for widespread adoption of MP3, and eventually creating an entirely new online format. First, Napster violated the MP3 patents held by the Fraunhofer Institute. Second, Napster violated music copyright law. So, why is MP3 widely and freely available, today?

The father of MP3 says,

> There were more and more people using this technology to store music on their hard discs. The idea was [originally] that encoders

would be much more expensive. … In, I think it was '97, some Australian student bought professional grade — from our point of view — encoding software for MP3 from a small company in Germany. He paid with a stolen credit card number from Taiwan. He looked at the software, found that we had used some Microsoft internal application programming interface … racked everything up into an archive and wired some Swedish side, [and] put that to a U.S. university FTP site together with a read-me file saying, "This is freeware thanks to Fraunhofer." He gave away our business model. We were completely not amused. We tried to hunt him down. We told everybody, "This is stolen software so don't distribute it," but still the business model to have expensive encoders and cheap decoders [was] done. From that time on, we reduced the cost for encoders.

When we found out that people used our technology to do unauthorized distribution of music over the Net — that was not our intention, very clearly. I have to say, I don't say that everything the music industry does is correct or good, but still I think we should have respect for the work of the artists and everybody involved and it's only fair that they get paid for it. It was in '97 when I got the impression that the avalanche was rolling and no one could stop it anymore. But even then I still sometimes have the feeling like is this all a dream or is it real, so it's clearly beyond the dreams of earlier times.*

MP3 was simply too successful for its own good. And, the patents ran out.

A GOOD IDEA GETS COPIED (ADVANCED)

The Fraunhofer Institute's lossy compression algorithm was such a good idea that subsequent standards groups copied it. For example, the Joint Photographic Experts Group created the JPEG standard for compressing pictures in 1992. JPEG is not only the defacto standard for the Internet, but also for most manufacturers of cameras. And like MP3, users can control quality and file size by selecting the level of quantization.

Unlike MP3, however, photographs and images are two-dimensional rather than unidirectional like sound. Images have a height and width dimension, so the compression algorithm must preprocess them in 2-D. For example, the 2-D cosine FFT is used in place of the simple cosine FFT. Once again, the cosine FFT is preferred because it compacts the signal into

---

* Ibid., Rose and Ganz.

fewer frequencies. Fewer frequencies mean fewer coefficients, which mean faster compression.

Secondly, psychoacoustic perception is different than psycho-visual perception, because ears are different organs than eyes. While the idea of pruning frequencies based on human perception is the same, the properties of sound are different than properties of light. Sound is one-dimensional, while sight is three-dimensional. Otherwise, the JPEG compression algorithm is very similar to the MP3 algorithm.

The JPEG compression algorithm should look familiar to the reader, because it paraphrases the MP3 algorithm. Both algorithms perform the following steps:

1. Preprocess the signal according to domain-specific perceptual and psycho-filtering models.

2. Apply the FFT to convert from the time domain to the frequency domain.

3. Quantize the frequency domain signal by scaling and rounding.

4. Encode or otherwise compress and send or store the signal.

According to trichromatic theory, the human eye is sensitive to only three parameters: luminance Y, and chrominances Cb and Cr. Most people are familiar with the RGB (Red-Green-Blue) 0 to 255 scale, which is related to the psycho-visual scale Y-Cb-Cr through the following matrix transformation*:

$$\begin{bmatrix} Y \\ Cb \\ Cr \end{bmatrix} = \begin{bmatrix} 0.299 & 0.587 & 0.114 \\ -0.169 & -0.331 & 0.5 \\ 0.5 & -0.419 & -0.081 \end{bmatrix} \begin{bmatrix} R \\ G \\ B \end{bmatrix} + \begin{bmatrix} 0 \\ 128 \\ 128 \end{bmatrix}$$

The inverse transformation is also a matrix multiplication:

$$\begin{bmatrix} R \\ G \\ B \end{bmatrix} = \begin{bmatrix} 1.0 & 0.0 & 1.402 \\ 1.0 & -0.344 & -0.714 \\ 1.0 & 1.772 & 0.0 \end{bmatrix} \left(\begin{bmatrix} Y \\ Cb \\ Cr \end{bmatrix} - \begin{bmatrix} 0 \\ 128 \\ 128 \end{bmatrix} \right)$$

---

* Neelamani, Ramesh, Ricardo de Queiroz, Zhigang Fan, Sanjeeb Dash, and Richard G. Baraniuk. (2005). JPEG Compression History Estimation for Color Images. https://scholarship.rice.edu/bitstream/handle/1911/20147/Nee2005Jul1JPEGCompre.PDF;sequence=1

Instead of sampling tones in music, JPEG samples Y, Cb, and Cr in an image, and then transforms 8×8 (or 16×16) pixel blocks into two-dimensional frequency domain frequencies using the familiar cosine FFT algorithm.

Psycho-visuals Y, Cb, and Cr correspond to planes, and each is subject to the same treatment during compression:

1. Split each plane into 8×8 (or 16×16) non-overlapping blocks and transform each block using the two-dimensional cosine FFT algorithm.

2. Quantize the coefficients of the frequency domain signal and round off as before:

$$Q = \text{round}\left(\frac{\text{Coefficient}}{q}\right)q$$

3. Optionally encode or further compress the signal for efficient transmission.

The decompression algorithm runs through the same steps on each plane in reverse order:

1. Decompress (reverse Huffman code) to extract the signal.

2. Invert the 8×8 (or 16×16) frequency domain blocks into 2-D spatial domain blocks by computing the inverse cosine FFT.

3. Apply the transformation from Y-Cb-Cr back into RGB.

4. Round off pixels to guarantee they lie in the range 0 to 255.

Image quality degrades as the compression algorithm increases quantification. This shows up in an image as pixilation and poor resolution. It is the quantizer that removes information and results in lossy compression. Note the formula for quantization contains divisor q. Increasing q increases compression but introduces distortion.

A more sophisticated quantizer combines psycho-visual perception cues and scaling to get the best of both worlds—compression and resolution. For example, the human eye is less sensitive to high-frequency distortions at the edges of an image block. If q is replaced by a matrix of q values such that greater scaling occurs along edges than near the center of an image, the image appears to be of higher quality than it actually is. The quantizer essentially quantizes higher frequencies more than lower frequencies. This produces additional lossy compression with minimal perceived psycho-visual loss. These and other tricks have been used to improve image compression beyond the basic JPEG standard.

MOVING JPEG IMAGES

FFT conversion followed by quantization is quick enough that the same idea used in JPEG can be used in video, but with some enhancements to accommodate frame-to-frame changes in moving pictures. After all, a video is simply consecutive still images, whereby the next frame is a modification of the current frame. But the required bandwidth is much greater, so we have to be even more ingenious. For example, a video containing 1920×1080 pixels, refreshed 24 times per second, in 16-bit color consumes 796 Mb/s of bandwidth. High-definition TV (HDTV) consumes twice this amount!

What other psycho-visual filtering might a video recorder do to reduce the burden beyond JPEG compression? Each frame can be compressed using the 2-D cosine FFT, quantized by scaling and rounding off, and smoothed by interpolation, but what else can be done? Sequencing a series of JPEG frames across time produces compressed MPEG video by combining the JPEG algorithm with additional steps to smooth out frame-to-frame changes.

MPEG depends on the fact that even high-performance motion content such as a speeding car or falling body contains pixels that change relatively slowly frame-to-frame. That is, most of the pixels that appear next are very similar to previously displayed pixels. Thus, MPEG treats frames the same or differently, depending on video content. An *I-frame* forms a baseline image and a *P-frame* forms a prediction of what a future frame will contain assuming pixels move in a direction established by comparing frames. That is, P-frames are predictions based on the difference between frames at time t and time t-1.

For example, frames containing a speeding car are likely to move in the direction of the car. Therefore, the MPEG algorithm can predict the state of adjacent pixels by interpolation. This is called *block matching*, because it works by comparing 8×8 or 16×16 blocks in I-frames and extrapolating what is likely to appear next. The P-frames and I-frames are compared and their differences recorded. Compression of the difference takes fewer bits of information than compression of entire frames.

If, however, the prediction is wrong, the algorithm must fall back on compressing full frames. The process of prediction starts over when a prediction fails.

Once again, descendants of MP3, JPEG, and MPEG lossy compression algorithms have made improvements over the years, but the basic idea of combining psycho-something with cosine FFT and quantization has stood the test of time. It is a basic technique that began with German researchers willing to give up perfection for very good approximations of perfection. Sometimes, 80% is good enough.

THE STORY OF ZIP

What if lossy compression simply won't do? Is Huffman compression sufficient or is there a better way to compress sounds and pictures without loss of information? This is the story of pioneering attempts to build a better mousetrap for compression. It starts with good intensions, but unfortunately has a bad ending.

Phil Katz (1962–2000) was found dead in a hotel room on April 14, 2000 at the age of 37. According to an article in the Milwaukee Journal Sentinel, Katz died with an empty bottle of peppermint schnapps in his arms,

> [W]hen he was found dead April 14, Phil Katz was slumped against a nightstand in a south side hotel, cradling an empty bottle of peppermint schnapps. The genius that built a multimillion-dollar software company known worldwide for its pioneering "zip" files had died of acute pancreatic bleeding caused by chronic alcoholism. He was alone, estranged long ago from his family and a virtual stranger to employees of his own company, PKWare Inc. of Brown Deer. It was an ignominious end for a man who created one of the most influential pieces of software in the world – PKZip – and it attracted the attention not only of the techno-faithful but of the mainstream press across the nation.
>
> Katz's inventions shrink computer files 50% to 70% to conserve precious space on hard disks. His compression software helped set a standard so widespread that "zipping" – compressing a file – became a part of the lexicon of PC users worldwide.
>
> But the riches his genius produced were no balm for what had become a hellish life of paranoia, booze and strip clubs. Toward the end, Katz worked only sporadically, firing up his computer

late at night, while filling his days with prodigious bouts of drinking and trysts with exotic dancers.*

Every personal computer user knows about PKZip—the utility for compressing any file to save storage space or speed transmission. But very few users know that Zip evolved from Katz's pioneering work. PKZip was invented decades after Huffman compression, so why is PKZip used while Huffman compression is not? Why is PKZip superior to Huffman compression?

Consider the US Declaration of Independence as a simple example. It is 1,311 words in length, but only 538 words are unique. Figure 6.2 shows how these 538 words are distributed. The most frequent words are "the," "of," and "to," and the least frequent words are "sacred," "fortunes," and "each." The Huffman algorithm uses the frequency of occurrence to replace each word by its corresponding code word. High-frequency words have shorter code words, which is the secret as to why Huffman compression reduces file size. But here is the catch—a table or dictionary of code words and their corresponding clear text word must be constructed and kept for decompression to put the compressed signal back into its original form. This table consumes memory space as well, reducing the compression ratio.

Figure 6.2 shows a sharp decline in frequency of unique words occurring in the Declaration of Independence. Low frequency and short words reduce compression ratio. If the clear text word is as short as its code word, there is no compression. Three-hundred eighty-three of the 528 words (72.5%) occur only once, and the most frequent words, "the" and "of" are nearly as short as their code words. Nonetheless, Huffman dictionary and code word file are compressed into approximately 3,678 characters instead of 7,996 characters (2.17 ratio). This can be considered a goal for any other compression algorithm, because the Huffman compression algorithm is considered optimal.

In practice, however, the Huffman algorithm has limitations. First and foremost, it requires two passes over the uncompressed file—one pass to obtain frequencies, and a second pass to replace clear text with code

* Hawkins, Lee, Jr. (2000). The Short, Tormented Life of Computer Genius Phil Katz. *JSOnline*, May 21, 2000. https://web.archive.org/web/20071221103157/http://www2.jsonline.com/news/state/may00/katz21052000a.asp

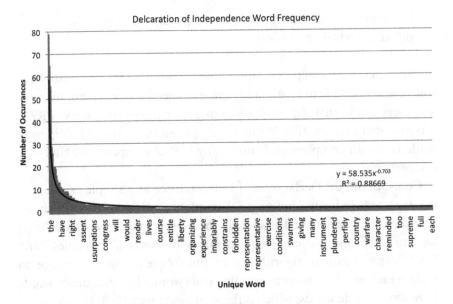

FIGURE 6.2 Words in the US Declaration of Independence obey a long-tailed power law according to Zipf's law.

words. Second, the code word itself can become long, because the algorithm assigns longer code words to least frequent clear text words.

As so often happens in the real world, PKZip is better in practice than theory, while Huffman is better in theory than practice.

Huffman and LZW, and its descendants like PKZip, belong to a class of *dictionary compression* algorithms. Instead of directly compressing symbols in a file, redundant strings in the file are replaced by pointers to a dictionary containing the redundant strings or symbols. Compression is the result of replacing long strings with short pointers and non-redundant copies stored in the dictionary. Welch set out to improve on Huffman and LWZ lossless compression by noting limitations of Huffman compression:

1. The algorithm must know the frequency of occurrence of every symbol in the file before any code word can be assigned.

2. Decompression is similarly burdened by variable-length code words.

LZW is a single-pass algorithm that builds the dictionary as it parses the file, starting with a dictionary containing strings of length one, and repeating the following until done:

1. Find the longest string in the dictionary that matches the current file input string.

2. If found, replace the found string with the dictionary index.

3. If not found, create a new string entry in the dictionary and replace the found string with the new dictionary index.

Decompression is obvious: simply construct an uncompressed file by replacing compressed file indexes with the strings fetched from the dictionary according to their indexes. The compressed string of code words is scanned to find a corresponding clear text word. The replacement clear text word can be of any length and is not restricted to single words.

The LZW algorithm was actually one innovation in a chain of innovations, L77, L78, etc., each improving on earlier versions. For example, the patented image format known as GIF employed an early version of LZW.* Moreover, Welch was employed by Sperry Research Center, which patented his derivative algorithm. Eventually, this complicated Phil Katz's life, and may have contributed to his death. Katz formed PKWARE Inc., whose products borrowed heavily from LZW and derivatives. In 1988, PKWARE was sued for copyright and trademark infringement by System Enhancement Associates (SEA)—maker of compression software called ARC.

According to Wikipedia,

> The SEA vs. PKWARE dispute quickly expanded into one of the largest controversies the BBS[†] world had ever seen. The suit by SEA angered many shareware users who perceived that SEA was a "large, faceless corporation" and Katz was "the little guy." In fact, at the time, both SEA and PKWARE were small home-based companies. However, the community largely sided with Katz, because SEA was attempting to retroactively declare the ARC file format to be closed and proprietary. Katz received positive publicity by releasing the APPNOTE.TXT specification, documenting the Zip file format, and declaring that the Zip file format would always be free for competing software to implement. The net result was that the ARC format quickly dropped out of common use as the

---

* https://mashable.com/2012/10/19/animated-gif-history/#Rl0HeBfSwiqO
† BBS—Bulletin Board System—was a popular bulletin board site in the early years of the Internet.

predominant compression format that bulletin board systems used for their file archives, and after a brief period of competing formats, the Zip format was adopted as the predominant standard.*

Katz lost the case brought against him, but his legal problems did not end there. Adoption of LZW and its variants was further suppressed by other commercial entities. It continued to spread, nonetheless. The rich and complicated history of Zip can be found at the Engineering and Technology History Wiki,

> Both the LZ77 and LZ78 algorithms grew rapidly in popularity, spawning many variants ... Most of these algorithms have died off since their invention, with just a handful seeing widespread use today including DEFLATE, LZMA, and LZX. Most of the commonly used algorithms are derived from the LZ77 algorithm. This is not due to technical superiority, but because LZ78 algorithms became patent-encumbered after Sperry patented the derivative LZW algorithm in 1984 and began suing software vendors, server admins, and even end users for using the GIF format without a license... The patent issues surrounding LZW have since subsided, as the patent on the LZW algorithm expired in 2003. Despite this, the LZW algorithm has largely been replaced and is only commonly used in GIF compression. There have also been some LZW derivatives since then but they do not enjoy widespread use either and LZ77 algorithms remain dominant.
>
> Another legal battle erupted in 1993 regarding the LZS algorithm. LZS was developed by Stac Electronics for use in disk compression software such as Stacker. Microsoft used the LZS algorithm in developing disk compression software that was released with MS-DOS 6.0 that purported to double the capacity of a hard drive. When Stac Electronics found out its intellectual property was being used, it filed suit against Microsoft. Microsoft was later found guilty of patent infringement and ordered to pay Stac Electronics $120 million in damages minus $13.6 million awarded in a countersuit finding that Microsoft's infringement was not willful. Although Stac Electronics v. Microsoft had a

---

* https://en.wikipedia.org/wiki/Phil_Katz

large judgment, it did not impede the development of Lempel-Ziv algorithms as the LZW patent dispute did. The only consequence seems to be that LZS has not been forked into any new algorithms.

Thom Henderson released the first commercially successful archive format called ARC in 1985 through his company, System Enhancement Associates. ARC was especially popular in the BBS community, since it was one of the first programs capable of both bundling and compressing files and it was also made open source. The ARC format uses a modification to the LZW algorithm to compress data. A man named Phil Katz noticed ARC's popularity and decided to improve it by writing the compression and decompression routines in assembly language. He released his PKARC program as shareware in 1987 and was later sued by Henderson for copyright infringement. He was found guilty and forced to pay royalties and other penalties as part of a cross-licensing agreement. He was found guilty because PKARC was a blatant copy of ARC; in some instances even the typos in the comments were identical.

Phil Katz could no longer sell PKARC after 1988 due to the cross-licensing agreement, so in 1989 he created a tweaked version of PKARC that is now known as the ZIP format. As a result of its use of LZW, it was considered patent-encumbered and Katz later chose to switch to the new IMPLODE algorithm. The format was again updated in 1993, when Katz released PKZIP 2.0, which implemented the DEFLATE algorithm as well as other features like split volumes. This version of the ZIP format is found ubiquitously today, as almost all .zip files follow the PKZIP 2.0 format despite its great age.*

The story of Zip is another story of deviant innovation. But this time, it killed the innovator.

COMMENT

Compression technology began with Huffman.

It has played a major role in the widespread adoption of electronic communications over the past 50 years. Compression may not seem like a revolutionary technology because it is hidden deep within the infrastructure of modern living, but it is and was a major enabler. Gary Stix writes

---

* https://ethw.org/History_of_Lossless_Data_Compression_Algorithms

about Huffman in *Scientific American*, "[His] epiphany added Huffman to the legion of largely anonymous engineers whose innovative thinking forms the technical underpinnings for the accoutrements of modem living—in his case, from facsimile machines to modems and a myriad of other devices."[*]

It is perhaps no coincidence that early work on practical compression was done in Europe, because the Europeans had fewer resources, memory-limited computers, and a keen sense of minimalist engineering. Minimalism turned out to be an advantage, because compression is all about minimization. If a single bit could be saved, the Germans were the first to understand how to do it. While developing MP3, Brandenburg could test only 20 seconds of music at a time, because of limited computer time. This is likely to have made him not only prudent, but wiser than others.

The story of Zip follows a different thread of history from the story of MP3 and its descendants. Zip started from the groundbreaking work of Abraham Lempel (1936–), Jacob Ziv (1931–), and Terry Welch (1939–1988) begun in 1977. Lempel and Ziv, in particular, developed a method for compressing files without loss of information. Lempel, an Israeli computer scientist, and Ziv, an Israeli engineer, co-invented lossless data compression for Unix using a dictionary. Terry Archer Welch was an American computer scientist working independently from Lempel and Ziv. Welch improved on the LZ algorithm and popularized the LZW algorithm of Lempel, Ziv, and Welch, as described in a 1984 IEEE Computer article.[†]

So the evolution of compression technology has two tracks—one for lossless and another for lossy compression. When the human ear or eye can be fooled, it pays to delete information for the sake of smaller files. When our eyes and ears object, we find it necessary to keep every bit of information intact, but remove redundancy. Then, to assure the receiver of compressed information that it is correct, the sender must add back some redundancy in the form of error-correcting codes to combat noise.

Thus, we have,

$$\text{Signal} = \text{Information} - \text{Redundancy} + \text{Error} - \text{Correction}$$

[*] Stix, Gary (1991). Profile: David A. Huffman. *Scientific American* (Sept 1991), pp. 54–58. https://www.huffmancoding.com/my-uncle/scientific-american

[†] Welch, Terry A. (1984). A Technique for High-performance Data Compression. *IEEE Computer* (June 1984), pp. 8–19. https://www2.cs.duke.edu/courses/spring03/cps296.5/papers/welch_1984_technique_for.pdf

CHAPTER 7

Radio Is Dead—Long Live Radio

THE WIND AND RAIN had died down enough on November 22, 1963 for me to dash from the Physics building to the basement of Ag Hall, where the ALWAC 3E computer heated a converted classroom. The keyboard and "terminal" of the vacuum tube machine was a Western Union ASR-33 teletypewriter machine, complete with keyboard, paper tape punch/reader, and printer. Three cabinets full of tubes and wires formed a backdrop behind it. They gave off enough warmth to fend off the northwest storm brewing outside.

I sat in front of the keyboard in stunned silence. President John F. Kennedy was dead. The word spread like a disease across the globe at nearly the speed of light through a global network known as the telegraph and waves known as radio. Even before there was the Internet, communication was fast and global when it wanted to be. It had been that way forever, it seemed to me. Unfortunately, bad news travels fast.

Sometimes called the "Victorian Internet," the global telegraph network was more than a century old when I began using the teletypewriter to communicate with one of the earliest digital computers. Thomas Edison worked as a telegrapher before he became an inventor. He was one of the best. He was fluent in the binary code invented by Morse and Vail a century before Shannon's information theory caught up with practice. Dots and dashes are, after all, a form of binary coding that goes all the way back to physical semaphore signaling. Digital communication was almost

200 years old by 1963, but it was about to change more in the next 50 years than all the years before.

After Danish scientist Hans Christian Oersted (1777–1851) hacked together a demonstration of the effects of an electric current on a magnetic needle, telegraphy began an exponential ascent to global ubiquity not unlike the exponential ascent of the Internet in the twentieth century. Telegraphy amazed people in the nineteenth century because it illustrated action at a distance. How is it possible to deflect a needle or tap a bar magnet against a metal surface from miles away? It seemed like magic.

The telegraph enjoyed many of the same triumphs and suffered many of the failures of today's Internet. It brought us the first cybercrime in the form of front-running stock markets. It also brought us early encryption methods to prevent cybercrime. It was an aid to law enforcement, allowing them to "wire ahead" of trains carrying escaping bank robbers. It pioneered digital cash, so that money could be wired from anywhere to anywhere else. As the technology matured, machines like the teletypewriter keyboard/printer replaced error-prone human operators. These machines translated Morse code and its descendants into print and the reverse—keystrokes into binary codes. Luckily, Edison moved on to more profitable endeavors before automation replaced him!

It is significant in the history of technology that telegraphy was digital. The binary code of Samuel Morse evolved into ASCII (American Standard Code for Information Interchange), which evolved into Unicode (Universal Coded Character Set) and then UTF-8 (Unicode Transformation Format – 8 bit) in 2007, a descendant of Morse code currently used by the Internet.* On March 11, 1968, US President Lyndon B. Johnson required all computers purchased by the United States federal government to support ASCII. Today's Unicode websites and e-mail are backward compatible with ASCII. Telegraphy and the standards established before the teletypewriter perished are still alive in today's Internet!

I slowly began typing my computer program on the ALWAC 3E teletypewriter terminal while contemplating the future. Clearly an era had ended and with it the high hopes of an entire generation. What was going to happen to us? In hindsight, it was the beginning of phenomenal technical progress that even a college sophomore, with more computer experience than the average human, could ever have imagined. In less than a decade, two humans on the moon would communicate via signals sent

---

* https://en.wikipedia.org/wiki/UTF-8

between Earth and the surface of the moon. Not to mention the transforming changes precipitated by the wireless Internet. How was this possible? Action at a distance would play a big role in this transformation. Even more significant was the coming grand convergence:

While analog radio and telephony was dominant for a short period of history, the real communication revolution was about to merge all forms of electronic communication into one digital format—packet-switched digital, compactly expressed as a Fourier Transformed OFDM (Orthogonal Frequency-Division Multiplex) signal. Dominant analog had to go. Radio emerged in its place.

ACTION AT A DISTANCE

The Royal Society of London was perhaps the most prestigious scientific organization in the world in 1864 when James Clerk Maxwell (1831–1879) presented his paper containing 20 equations and 20 variables that consolidated the work of Hans C. Oersted (1777–1851), Carl F. Gauss (1777–1855), André M. Ampère (1775–1836), Michael Faraday (1791–1867), and others. It was a tour de force of speculation and controversy. In fact, it was not entirely correct and remained unverified for another 20 years. For one thing, Maxwell's equations were based on mechanical laws, not electromagnetic laws. Some historians suggest that Maxwell was not completely convinced of the existence of electromagnetism as we know it today, but rather he was attempting to explain the interaction of light with magnets in terms of mechanical phenomena.* Confirmation of Maxwell's equations was left up to another member of the Royal Society. In the end, his theory predicted the equivalence of light and electromagnetic waves. And pre-dated all early forms of electronic communication by decades.

The proof of the existence of electromagnetism as expressed in Maxwell's equations was left up to a young Heinrich Rudolf Hertz (1857–1894). Hertz had only recently moved to the University of Bonn—more for its beautiful setting on the Rhine than its scientific reputation. Life was good. He had two daughters, Johanna and Mathilda, and a wife named Elizabeth. His students adored him, and one colleague declared him a noble man and was charmed by his amiability. Nonetheless, the pain in his throat and nose was so intense he had all of his teeth pulled. He got hay fever treatments and went to health clinics seeking a cure. Nothing worked. All attempts to

---

* Sengupta, Dipak L. and Tapan K. Sarkar (2003). *Maxwell, Hertz, the Maxwellians and the Early History of Electromagnetic Waves.* John Wiley & Sons, February 2006. doi:10.1002/0471783021.ch5

cure what ailed him failed and he died a month after delivering his final lecture at the University. He was only 36 years old. If immortality is the impact one has on the world after leaving it, Hertz was immortal, because he turned Maxwell's theory of communication into practice. He was the pathfinder that led us to all forms of modern electronic communication. You might say he was the *father of the signal.*

Between 1865 and 1873, Maxwell had established the most important theoretical principles of the nineteenth century. Maxwell's equations established the equivalence of light with other forms of electromagnetism—waves that carry signals. Visible light is simply a small piece of the largely invisible electromagnetic spectrum that we can see. He even came close to estimating the correct speed of light. But it was only a brilliant theoretical result. Proving Maxwell right was the problem assigned to Heinrich Hertz by his advisor, Hermann von Helmholtz (1821–1894). Were the Maxwell equations valid? It would take Hertz most of his short life to demonstrate that Maxwell's equations accurately described reality.

Hertz demonstrated wireless transmission of a wireless signal using electromagnetic waves and confirmed the truth of Maxwell's equations. He ushered in radio.

The nineteenth century was a time of phenomenal progress in physics as far as it went toward describing what people could see, hear, touch, and measure. It was not as successful explaining things that could not be detected by human perception. It failed to anticipate the unseen world. In particular, it could not explain magnetism, light, and the hacking of the signal by inventors like Thomas Edison and Nikola Tesla. Before Maxwell and Hertz, communicating through thin air appeared to be magic. How could something act on something else without touching it, being seen or heard, and apparently traveling instantaneously through space?

Maxwell himself was not initially sure that electromagnetism fully explained "action at a distance." The prevailing theory of light and magnetic attraction at the time postulated a universe permeated by an invisible elastic solid—the *ether*—that propagated force across long distances. The ether was a kind of jello supporting waves of disturbances like ripples in a pond created by a thrown rock. Does a fish know it is in water? Do humans know they are swimming in an invisible sea of jello? Maxwell's equations are based on mechanical properties of mass, weight, and forces swimming through the unseen world of ether. Electromagnetic forces travel through this jello-like medium until they encounter a physical object that absorbs their kinetic energy. It is this sea in a vastly unseen world that supports the signal along a path from point A to point B anywhere in the universe. And Maxwell's equations described how it all worked.

Maxwell did not live to see his famous equations confirmed. He was dead long before they were even widely accepted by his peers. It was up to Hertz and the *Maxwellians*—George F. FitzGerald (1851–1901), Oliver J. Lodge (1851–1940), Oliver Heaviside (1850–1925), and others to carry on his work and turn theory into practice.* Their stories are the stories of radio and how the signal got physical. The Maxwellians pieced together the unseen electromagnetic world through a series of inventions, innovations, trials, and primitive successes. They were the founders of modern electronic communication long before it became the society-bending technology that permeates everyday life today.

Hertz built the first radio transmitter using a *spark gap oscillator*. This consisted of two 1-meter wires separated by a 7.5 mm spark gap, each wire connected at the other end to a 30 cm zinc ball serving as a capacitor (to charge the spark). Different sized balls provided different capacitance, which resulted in a spark sending out waves at different frequencies. Thus, he tuned the signal by changing zinc balls. This contraption incorporated the first antenna expressly designed for radio.

Hertz applied 20,000 volts to both sides, causing a spark and an oscillating standing wave to travel through the wires at approximately 50 Mhz, which is what a modern television station transmits, today. He constructed an LC (inductive-capacitive) circuit and antenna that resonated with the oscillations created by the spark. Incredible to people around him, these oscillations permeated the jello-like ether such that they could be sensed by another antenna with similar properties.

The receiver was even simpler. It consisted of a copper wire bent almost into a complete circle of diameter 7.5 cm. One end was pointed and the other end was rounded into a ball. An adjustment screw allowed Hertz to adjust the separation distance between the pointed end and the rounded end. The dimensions of this primitive receiver were purposely designed so the copper wire resonated at the same frequency as the transmitter. Electromagnetic waves from the transmitter induced a current in the receiver causing a discharge across the point-and-rounded ends of the circular antenna.

---

* Hunt, Bruce J. (1991). *The Maxwellians*. Cornell University Press. https://en.wikipedia.org/wiki/The_Maxwellians

Hertz demonstrated action at a distance when a distant antenna reso-nated at the same frequency as his primitive radio.

The global telegraph network was at its peak when Hertz showed how to replace it with a wireless network. He was in a position to disrupt a major industry. But, Hertz was a scientist, not a businessman with commercial interests. Even after confirming Maxwell's theory by experiments where Hertz both transmitted and received electromagnetic radiation—radio waves—he could find no practical applications! His visionary experiments did not lead to visionary business innovation.

But Hertz inspired others. Lodge, in particular, was more practically minded than either Maxwell or Hertz. He exploited the Maxwell–Hertz discoveries and made his own discoveries. Lodge is best remembered for the *coherer*—a device that could be tuned to detect a certain frequency of radio wave. The coherer was a tube containing metal filings and two electrodes separated by a gap. French inventor Édouard Eugène Désiré Branly (1844–1940) had previously noted that tubes filled with iron fil-ings resisted the flow of electricity until a current is applied to the elec-trodes, reducing resistance, and permitting current to flow. When current is applied to the coherer, the iron filings cohere or cling together, hence the name. Lodge devised a means of reversing the process to de-cohere the iron filings so the process of "rectifying" a signal could be repeated. Eventually crystals replaced the coherer in the 1920s. Amateur ham radio operators continued using crystal radios far into the twentieth century. But that is another story.

By the 1850s, the first global telecommunications system—the tele-graph—was successfully transmitting and receiving digital messages throughout the world. Thomas Edison and others incorporated many improvements to telegraphy as they were discovered, but the telegraph depended on wires and wires were expensive and prone to damage. The technological prize of the century would go to whoever was able to har-ness electromagnetic waves for telegraphy. In fact, Oliver Heaviside was mentored by one of the co-inventors of the Victorian telegraph. Sir Charles Wheatstone (1802–1875) took an interest in his education, which paid off much later when Heaviside became inspired by Maxwell's writings. The turning point for young Heaviside came about when he read Maxwell's 1873 "Treatise on Electricity and Magnetism." Heaviside suddenly became a different man, contributing many innovations to telegraphy and pre-relativistic science. He condensed 12 of the 20 Maxwell equations into four equations, which is the form we now call Maxwell's equations.

Heaviside's equations boiled electromagnetic theory down to a handful of well-known equations that form the basis of modern communication and computing technology. In fact, Albert Einstein called them the Maxwel–Heaviside equations. They are routinely used today to design antennae, radio, and television, and, of course, computers and modern wireless communication systems.

Signals are concise mathematical objects that obey the Maxwel-- Heaviside equations that describe electromagnetic radiation. These mathematical objects travel through vacuum, atmosphere, cable, glass fiber optics, and computer circuits in abeyance of the Maxwell–Heaviside equations. The realization that a fundamental physical phenomenon like electromagnetism and light conforms to rigorous mathematical equations is one of the supreme accomplishments of modern communication systems, and scientific thought, in general.

PHYSICAL INFORMATION

Crude devices were invented to tame electromagnetic radiation. The Maxwellians and their descendants eventually learned how to tune oscillations to specific frequencies and amplitudes. They refined sparks into transmitters and wires into antennae. They eventually learned how to amplify weak signals and discovered the ionized layer of the atmosphere called the ionosphere where radio signals bounced back to earth along an arc that permitted long-distance transmissions. The electromagnetic waves predicted by Maxwell were rapidly exploited to bring us radio, TV, and ultimately Wi-Fi and 5G.

How is information in the form of bits related to the physical transmission and reception of the signal? Information must be encoded in some property of a physical process to be able to transmit and receive it. The time taken by a photon to travel from point A to point B is itself a form of information. The frequency of an electromagnetic disturbance is information. The intensity of a sound is information, etc. These tangible properties of physical processes are used in clever ways to encode the less tangible information.

The process of systematically encoding a physical process so that it carries information in a rigorous and repeatable way is called *modulation*. The physical process underlying modulation is called a *carrier*. The reverse process, *demodulation*, recovers the information encapsulated by modulation and carried by the carrier process. Modulation, followed by demodulation, is routinely used in all forms of modern signal processing.

Most people have heard of AM and FM (Amplitude Modulation and Frequency Modulation) but few have heard of Reginald A. Fressenden (1866–1932), a Canadian inventor with hundreds of patents related to radio and sonar. Fressenden pressured Edison until the famous inventor hired him as an assistant at the Edison Machine Works, a subsidiary that installed underground electrical cables in New York City. But Fressenden did more than install cables under New York. He is best known for inventing AM radio and for the first broadcast of speech by radio in 1900, the first two-way telegraphic communication across the Atlantic Ocean in 1906, and technological improvements in receivers.

Amplitude modulation encodes binary ones and zeros as voltage levels or amplitudes of sine waves, see Figure 7.1. Similarly, FM encodes ones

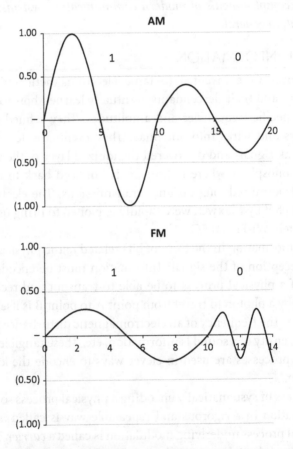

FIGURE 7.1 Amplitude modulation encodes zero and one using different amplitudes, and frequency modulation encodes zero and one using different frequencies.

and zeros as different frequencies. The pure sine wave is a carrier and modulation encodes information on top of the carrier. These are two of the simplest forms of modulation used to encode information in terms of a physical property. They are not the only forms. But they laid the foundation for innovative and clever forms of modulation described in this book. The path from Maxwell to Hertz to Fressenden to modern cellular telephony and the wireless Internet was not a straight line, however. There were detours.

A MISSTEP?

In the late 1980s, I lugged a small suitcase sized cellular telephone into the back seat of my car to keep me connected while I commuted between Corvallis and Beaverton, Oregon. It was an expensive piece of communication gear—one that very few people could afford. Luckily, my employer was paying for it. The commute was almost 90 minutes long, but the cost of a 90-minute wireless telephone call was prohibitive. So, I hardly ever used it. The brick-like telephone was the most advanced communication device one could buy in the 1980s.

The ubiquitous *smart phone* was at least two decades in the future for me, and millions of others. One reason was the immature technology of that time—there simply was no technology powerful enough to support digital telephony in 1988. But another, more damaging reason was the analog misstep. Cell phones existed for many decades before I got mine in 1988, but they were analog. Analog was a temporary detour on the road to ubiquitous wireless communication. For one thing, analog signals cannot be enhanced by software. For another thing, analog signals are much more difficult to filter. So the sooner an AM or FM signal can be converted into a digital signal, the better.

For most of the twentieth century, the signal was managed by two competing industries—the telecommunications and computing industries. They created separate and eventually convergent means of communicating information. The telecommunications industry promoted analog signaling through extremely clever and novel analog encoding, switching, and decoding machines. The computing industry, on the other hand, created extremely clever and novel digital encoding, switching, and decoding machines. The two eventually met (and clashed?) with the invention of the cell phone, and rise of the Internet.

The two kingdoms of signal processing would vie for supremacy until the Telecommunications Act of 1996 and the 1998 commercialization of the Internet demolished the difference. Some call it deregulation of the AT&T monopoly and liberation of the Internet. I call it the turning point that revolutionized global communication and computing. But first, let me review the rise of the analog cellular telephone that would set the stage for the wireless Internet of today.

KINGS OF ANALOG

Before the 1996 Telecommunications Act, the AT&T–Bell Labs combination was king of analog. These two organizations held a monopoly or near-monopoly on all forms of two-way electronic communication between consumers. The AT&T "natural monopoly" successfully staved off challenges from competitors like Carterfone and IBM for nearly a century. And, they were married to analog. But the rise of the digital computer was a different story. One of the critical events took place in the 1980s when the computer industry began to "infringe" on the AT&T-dominated communications industry.

Martin Cooper (1928–)—the *father of the cell phone*—started working for the Teletype Corporation in Chicago in 1954, but moved to Motorola—a car radio company—in the 1960s, where he worked on a police radio system for the Chicago Police Department. He was inspired by the 1931–1977 era Dick Tracy wrist radio that was similar to today's digital watch—only Dick Tracy was 70 years ahead of his time. In 1973, Motorola allocated $100 million to Cooper's team to develop the first cell phone. The race between Motorola—a computer company—and Bell Labs—a communications company—was on.

Cooper made the first call on a portable cell phone in April 1973 to his rival, Joel Engel, who was head of Bell Labs research. The prototype phone was the DynaTAC weighing 28 ounces. Bell Laboratories had introduced the idea of cellular communications in 1947 with the police car technology, but it was Motorola that first incorporated the technology into a portable device without the automobile as an accessory. The analog DynaTAC eventually sold for $4,000 and ran out of power in 30 minutes.

Forty-four years later, Martin Cooper had 8,000 Twitter followers online. In a 2017 interview, Cooper said this about the first call,

> The immediate feeling was relief that the demonstration worked. That first phone was painstakingly hand-assembled out of many hundreds of components. It was a testament to the skill and persistence of the team that did it that it worked at all. But it did

work. We didn't really celebrate until the FCC allowed Motorola to influence the standards that made portable phones possible and allowed competition to prevail in the wireless industry.*

But the real problem was: Cooper invented an analog cell phone. Analog machines cannot be programmed without changing hardware, while digital machine functionality is largely based on programmable software. Nonetheless it showed how a computer company rather than AT&T might dominate the future of communications. How prescient.

The march toward digital was slow and painful for the communications industry. It evolved over a period of two decades, denoted by generations, summarized in Table 7.1. It took the wireless telephony industry two decades to transition to packet-switched data, and another decade to adopt full Internet protocols. Even as I write this in 2018, the cellular signal is struggling to support video streaming. By 2020 streaming will be common, but even more significantly, most Internet access will be via wireless, including video. Generation 5, or 5G, may even spell the end of cable or fiber optic lines at the last mile. Cable and fiber will remain the preferred technology for long-haul lines, but may vanish at the doorstep to your office or house.

What began as an attempt to reach motorists in their car has emerged as the preferred way to access the global Internet. In Chapter 9, we return to the earlier problem of overcoming great distance by signaling at the quantum level. But for the next many decades, the combination of OFDM, QAM, and the Hertz radio will prevail as the main means of human-to-human communication. And the scale of deployment is unprecedented.

Never before has so many people been so connected by such a powerful signal. The radio may be dead, but the radio signal is still alive and evolving.

TABLE 7.1   Evolution of Cellular Telephony

Generation	Era	Speed	Main Features
1G	1980–1990	2.4 kbps	Analog voice
2G	1991–2000	64 kbps	Analog voice, digital data, SMS
3G	2000–2010	2.0 mbps	Analog voice, digital packet data
4G (LTE)	2010–2020	100 mbps	Internet protocols, Wi-Fi
5G	2020–?	1–2 gbps	Interactive multimedia (video, tele-presence)

---

* http://www.motorola-fans.com/2017/06/motorola-fans-exclusive-interview-with-martin-cooper.html

IT'S INFRASTRUCTURE, STUPID!

Building an inexpensive, powerful programmable handset is one-half of the solution. The other half is the infrastructure required to support transmission of handset signals to other handsets. Radio has a limited range, especially if it must avoid blotting out other radio waves. The mobility of a cellular telephone challenged the 100-year tradition of station-to-station calling established by the telegraph. Person-to-person telegraphy without wires became an obsession long before it became a reality. Bell Labs set about to expand AT&T's dominance over electronic communication through a system of relays, called a *cellular network*.

The idea of personal wireless communication originated in the military. Starting in 1940, hand-held "walkie-talkie" transmitter/receiver radios were deployed on the battlefield for the first time. A mesh of transmit-and-receive stations covering a battlefield made perfect sense as long as the battlefield was not too large. Messages could manually hop from walkie-talkie to walkie-talkie via trained operators. This, of course, would not work in a commercial setting. Hopping had to be automated.

The feasibility of erecting expensive relay towers about every 3–5 miles across the entire continent to make a local or long-distance call seemed far-fetched and highly unlikely in Dick Tracy's era. But this is exactly what the research staff at Bell Labs proposed over 65 years ago. In a 1947 memo written by Douglas H. Ring (1907–2000) to Bell Labs management, Ring and W. Rae Young (1915–2008) proposed a cellular network made up of *hexagonal cells* for use by wireless phones in cars. Cars can haul large devices and they can also provide power, hence the focus on automobile mobility. Rae was a versatile musician who played the piano, clarinet, cello, and bass. His suggestion that cells be hexagonal may have come from an artistic sense of symmetry, or the mathematical fact that hexagonal cells maximize the coverage of the surrounding area. The hexagon partitioned 360 degrees into 60-degree pie-sliced regions. The Ring–Young memo set off a steady stream of innovations.

Amos Joel (1940–2008) invented and patented the handoff between towers (patent number 3,663,762 granted in 1972). As a connected car moves out of range of one cell into the range of another, the system must be able to switch seamlessly from one cell to the other. According to his sister, "As a boy, he wired a communication system for his friends, using old phone equipment that was left behind in vacant apartments and building a crude switchboard with knife switches, only to be caught by a repairman."*

---

* https://www.nytimes.com/2008/10/28/technology/28joel.html

The modern cell phone contains three numbers: its telephone number, the device identity, and the carrier identity. Regardless of where you are, these numbers are paired with the nearest cell tower so a carrier point-of-presence switch can find the handset. Incredibly, a call placed from another handset is routed through towers, landlines, and wireless connections to the tower currently paired with the phone. This is made possible by a collection of technologies, many of which have been described in this book.

Phillip T. Porter (1930–2011) improved signal reception by noting that placing a directional antenna at one corner of the hexagonal cell instead of the center worked better. Handsets are paired with the strongest tower signals. This idea was subsequently applied to Bluetooth and Wi-Fi, as well. Porter also invented the dial-then-send protocol to save bandwidth. The handset is offline while you enter the number, and online only after the number is entered.

Richard H. Frenkiel (1943–) showed how to split cells into smaller cells to accommodate high-density areas. He made cellular signaling scalable to many users. Joel S. Engel (1936–) led the group and answered the phone when Cooper called in 1983 from the Motorola phone—notifying the Bell Labs team that they had been scooped.

Frenkiel and Engel put the word *cell* in cellular. Working with a team of nearly 200 Bell Lab engineers, Engel and Frenkiel developed a concept that multiplied the capacity of each channel by 1,000. Their system divided cities up into small coverage areas called cells. A land-based network tracked cars (or other mobile units) within cells and switched calls from cell to cell as the unit moved. With this system, Frenkiel and Engel shaped the basic cellular system architecture and solved complex problems such as how cellular systems locate vehicles and hand off calls from cell to cell as vehicles move.

Engel and Frenkiel's work led to a series of proposals to the Federal Communications Commission (FCC) in the 1970s and became the foundation for the cellular system, which revolutionized mobile communications and made today's convenient cellular services readily available. In 1987, Frenkiel and Engel were awarded the Alexander Graham Bell Medal of the IEEE for exceptional contributions to the advancement of telecommunications. In 1994, the pair received National Medals of Technology from President Clinton.

Following the proposals to the FCC, Frenkiel went on to lead the team of Bell Labs engineers who wrote specifications for and refined the cellular system architecture, reported on system tests to the FCC, and helped plan the first wave of cellular systems for deployment in the early 1980s.*

The infrastructure started out analog, but eventually it would become digital. The kings of communication lived and breathed analog, but the future was digital.

KINGS OF COMPUTING

The kings of computing lived in a parallel universe with different motivations and a different vision. They began with the premise that communication was an extension of computing. Unlike Bell Labs, their vision was of computer-to-computer or computer-to-people communication taking place at the speed of a machine. This machine-centric point of view also motivated much of the early Internet and by the 1980s it was spilling over into the communication space. The two industries were on a collision course.

A landmark invention occurred in 1983, when Texas Instruments created the single-chip DSP (Digital Signal Processor). This chip implemented the FFT (Fast Fourier Transform) and other signal processing functions in one device for the first time. FFT was the missing link between digital computation and analog communication. It enabled digital communication as we know it, today—whether between machines or people. When E.T. called home, it must have been on a digital device using the FFT, or the alien equivalent.

As described in an earlier chapter, the first jolt came when the Carterfone decision allowed AT&T competitors to use the monopoly's telephone lines. The second jolt occurred in 1984 when AT&T was broken up into seven regional "Baby Bells," thus ending the 50-year-old monopoly. Highlights of the historic 19-page "final judgment" that legally and financially divided Western Electric and AT&T into Bell Labs and seven companies are summarized below:

The Bell Operating Companies (BOC) or "Baby Bells" must continue to interoperate even though they are legally and financially separate entities.

---

* http://lemelson.mit.edu/resources/richard-h-frenkiel-and-joel-s-engel

They must cooperate and compete at the same time. Cooperation means sharing infrastructure but not financial data or corporate strategy.

The BOCs shall operate in non-overlapping regions called exchange areas. This may have seemed like a good idea at the time, but eventually the Gause's competitive exclusion principle sets in and an oligopoly or monopoly forms. Today we have only four of the seven telephone companies still standing.

A BOC may provide, but not manufacture, customer premises equipment. This rule was aimed at Western Electric, which made nearly all of the handsets. It is irrelevant today as Apple Inc. and Samsung—computer companies and not communication companies—make the majority of handsets.

All intellectual property owned by AT&T shall be transferred to separated BOCs. As of this writing, all of the intellectual property once commanded by AT&T has expired and dissipated. Perhaps Qualcomm and Broadcom—predominantly computer companies—come closest to owning the intellectual property used by manufacturers.

AT&T shall not engage in electronic publishing over its transmission facilities. This rule was aimed at separating carriers from content. AT&T should not use its dominance in providing communication services to also dominate publishing of content such as books, music, and movies.

This decree defined the Baby Bells as Interexchange Carriers (IECs) in contrast to a Local Exchange Carrier (LEC). This created a three-tier system: the old AT&T with its long-lines (long-distance lines), the regional Baby Bells that relied on both long lines and short lines, and the LECs that delivered telephone services to homes and offices. To complete a call from California to New York, a consumer had to cross all three boundaries with different rules, tariffs, and restrictions. This inefficient and outdated system had to undergo radical change in the digital era.

The Telecommunications Act of 1996 directly addressed the "natural monopoly" of the old tiered system by recognizing the inevitable convergence of computing and communicating. In particular, it aimed to deregulate the Baby Bell hodgepodge of companies so that the Internet could flourish. According to the Federal Communications Commission (FCC), the goal of the law was to let anyone enter any communications business—to let any communications business compete in any market against any other. Highlights of the deregulation are:

Interconnectivity: LECs could use the IEC network and vice versa. This was perhaps the most important change, because it forced the LECs to let the IECs complete a call over the "last mile" connecting consumers to long-lines. And it forced the IECs to allow LECs to use their long-lines to make long-distance calls. The communications world suddenly became flat.

Any and all Baby Bells may provide long-distance service. This is a consequence of the first rule change. Not only could a Baby Bell compete over the long-lines, new entrants immediately and with little cost became national (and eventually international) service providers. It is difficult in the Internet era to think there was a time when a telecommunications connection was restricted to a region or country. Today it is as easy to connect with someone in China as it is someone in Europe or the USA.

LECs and IECs are required to share access, hence the legislation indirectly created massive "telecom hotels" containing massive switching equipment and massive access to the Internet. While this seemed like a good idea at the time, the creation of massive telecom hotels has become the number one physical vulnerability of the Internet. If a terrorist wishes to do physical harm to the Internet, an attack on a heavily connected telecom hotel will do the most damage.

Telecommunication companies were barred from providing content such as e-mail, videos, etc. [This is likely to change.] This provision began to crumble when Comcast merged with NBC and entered the content production business while simultaneously seeking to dominant cable TV and Internet service provision. This may eventually lead to anti-trust action, but at the time this was written, America was in a pro-big-business mood, politically.

The act provides for digital TV broadcasting, cable TV, communications decency, and miscellaneous billing practices. On the surface, this may seem to be a messy detail, but with the rise of hacking and online crime, it has become one of the (few) tools for law enforcement to catch and prosecute Internet criminals.

The foregoing rules are rather extensive, and yet the 1996 Telecommunications Act left out many provisions that may impact the signal going forward. There is no mention of wireless cellular telephony. The iPhone had not yet been invented in 1996 and the exponential spread of smart phones had not begun until approximately 1999. Communications via TCP/IP and cellular telephony was still in its infancy. In hindsight, the wireless segment of the industry would overwhelm the landline segment. Who knew?

Net neutrality was an unknown in 1996 so there is no mention of net neutrality. Consumers pressured the Internet Service Providers (ISP) to remain neutral, meaning the ISP did not provide more bandwidth to one e-commerce business than another or re-direct traffic flow for monetary gain. Net neutrality remained in place for a time, but in 2017–2018 the FCC ruled in favor of ISP's throttling or otherwise directing Internet traffic flow to their advantage. As I write this in 2018, the controversy continues, and the FCC ruling may be reversed by the time you read this.

The impact of highly concentrated telecom hotel facilities on national security was not addressed or even anticipated. The best way to make the Internet run smoothly is to reduce time delays and friction between service providers. The signal should be able to quickly and easily jump from AT&T to Verizon to T-Mobile, to Amazon.com. One way to guarantee this is to co-locate switching equipment in large data centers such as the one at 57 Hudson Street near the financial district of New York or One Wilshire Boulevard in Los Angeles that connects California to Asia. The virtues of centralization at key hubs throughout the nation may have clouded policy-maker's vision. These (and other) large co-location buildings make easy targets for terrorism.

The Act has been roundly criticized for decreasing competition rather than increasing it. Critics called it an "insult to the dreams of Jefferson, Washington, Mill, Madison, DeToqueville, and Brandeis."* Critics of government intervention in the communications and computing industries argue that such regulation stifles innovation and technological progress. Regardless, the 1996 Telecommunications Act accelerated the "Grand Convergence"—a consolidation of all kinds of signals into a universal standard.

Grand convergence is upon us, now. We call it 5G.

COMMENT

The history of the signal is long and winding, but we can now see the trend as a transition from analog to digital, and from digital to an error-correcting, compressed, mathematical function. The major wired and wireless services implement well-known OFDM/QAF techniques, cyclic redundancy checking such as Reed–Solomon or a Turbo code, and packet routing rather than circuit switching. The major differences among a cell phone, Internet, or wireless connection is performance, not encoding: Bluetooth is short range, Wi-Fi and cellular are medium range, and cable/fiber are long range. Power consumption varies along with range,

---

* https://en.wikipedia.org/wiki/Telecommunications_Act_of_1996

but the mathematical definition of the signal is the same for all. Grand convergence means we can trade off cost and performance without losing interoperability across devices and across all types of media—text, audio, image, and video.

By 2020, the emergence of 5G will be in full flower, and provide competition to infrastructure industries that rely on expensive wires to deliver content such as cable TV. While the long-haul lines are likely to remain safe against disruption, the challenger is warming up in the pitcher's bullpen. The fifth-generation signal is the final step in a grand convergence that merges cable, Wi-Fi, Bluetooth, Internet, and cellular communication into one technology. 5G is about to become (as of 2019) the dominant platform for all earthly forms of communications.

Radio is dead. Long live radio, in its many new incarnations.

CHAPTER 8

128 Ears to Listen

S ITTING IN THE CROWN and Anchor English Pub in Monterey, California, the city where Gary Kildall (1942–1994) developed the first high-level programming language for microprocessors, called PL/M and the first operating system called CP/M, I recalled the good old days when Gary was about to become what Bill Gates became—rich and famous. In 1994, the Crown and Anchor was a biker bar with a different name, tough reputation, and scruffy customers. After playing his last game of pool in the below-sidewalk-level hall Gary allegedly fell over, and died of blunt force trauma to his head three days later. The man who started the personal computer operating system industry and established the first operating system standard of the personal computer era was dead at the age of 52.

Many years after the death of Kildall, the pool table was replaced by a dining room and the biker bar was turned into the British Pub I enjoy, today. The Crown and Anchor is a popular tourist hangout, but unfortunately, most people don't know that computer pioneer and software innovator Kildall died from injuries suffered here. Most people probably don't know he even existed. And yet, Kildall saw further into the future than most of his contemporaries, including Bill Gates. [Gates purchased Microsoft's first operating system, MS-DOS rather than inventing it. MS-DOS was a CP/M knockoff.] Sometimes it pays to be second, rather than first.

My thoughts now turn to that era of recombinant innovation, where innovators like Kildall pieced together bits of technology to create an entirely new and exciting industry—the personal computer industry.

Hobbyists and serious technologists like Gary Kildall and Bill Gates combined low-cost microcomputers, low-cost diskette drives, and novel operating systems software with traditional keyboards, printers, and TV monitors to fabricate the earliest personal computers. They borrowed much from existing technology, but added something new right at the point in time when the computer industry was dominated by a handful of mainframe and minicomputer manufacturers like IBM, GE, Honeywell, DEC, and others. The computer industry was about to radically change right at its peak. Who would think to challenge these giants?

The domination of the computer industry in the 1970s by large companies with large and expensive products is exactly why these personal computer pioneers dared to challenge the incumbents. Boomer generation innovators like Kildall, Gates, Jobs, and Wozniak were motivated by the desire to topple the big companies with their big government and big company customers. Back then, only a select few—the technological elite—had access to the power of computing. The challengers argued that this had to change.

The personal computer visionaries of the 1970–1980s era clearly understood the *white space* left open by huge mainframe computer companies on one end of the spectrum and computer hobbyists building their own home computers on the other end. In 1975, no products filled this niche. Gary Kildall was one of the first to fill this white space by inventing and selling the first microcomputer operating system, CP/M (Control Program for Microcomputers). He showed that it was possible to build a billion-dollar company out of inexpensive hardware in a market dominated by giants. Kildall's early success paved the road ahead for companies that nobody ever heard of like Microsoft, Apple, and Oracle. It was like opening up the Northwest Passage to European sailors in the 1700s.

At the time this was written, the communications industry stands on the precipice of another transformational era very much like the personal computer industry in 1976. This industry is dominated by a handful of incumbents like AT&T, Verizon, Xfinity, Cox, Vodafone, T-Mobile, Orange, and China Mobile. These carriers deliver information through proprietary technologies with names like CDMA (Code-Division Multiple Access), GSM (Global Systems for Mobile communication), LTE (Long Term Evolution), and the G's—3G, 4G, and 5G. A smart phone designed for one technology does not work on another technology. The alphabet soup of technologies locks consumers into one vendor or another with little hope of interoperability.

But communications alphabet soup ends with the introduction of 5G. Total convergence is possible—and inevitable—with 5G. The only problem is, nobody is sure what 5G is (circa 2020) any more than Gary Kildall knew what personal computing was in 1976. 5G seems to be a marketing term for any technology that can accommodate one hundred times more devices, one hundred times more bandwidth, lower power, and lower latency. In addition, it has to be 100% compatible with the Internet protocols and work everywhere on the planet.

To turn a marketing term into reality, technologists are piecing together existing and new technology to create an entirely new and exciting industry—the 5G-and-beyond communications industry. What exactly will they cobble together is uncertain, but it is clearly the case that 5G communications mark the beginning, not the end, of innovation in signal transmission and reception. The signal is about to undergo a change on par with the invention of personal computers and smart phones.

EMERGENT 5G

The previous chapters describe the progression of communications theory from the invention of the radio through increasingly sophisticated error-correction algorithms to highly mathematical and effective exploitation of the electromagnetic spectrum, eventually ending with OFDM/QAM—Orthogonal Frequency-Division Modulation/Quadrature Amplitude Method—a mouthful. Technologists have found ways to broaden bandwidth to encode digital bits by slicing and dicing a band of frequencies into many smaller frequency bands so that bits can be transmitted and received in parallel. The "higher frequency, wider band" approach exploits QAM as described in the previous chapter.

But, higher frequencies present other problems.

Intuitively, higher frequencies are ripe for exploitation in OFDM/QAM systems because high-frequency wide-band signals can be sliced and diced into more parallel channels. Think of a high-frequency wave as containing many more peaks and valleys than a low-frequency wave. Each peak can carry a bit of information, so the more peaks per second, the more bits per second. Therefore, higher frequency equals more bits per second. Now, combine many high-frequency carrier waves together such that each carries many bits per second, and the result is a high-speed parallel signal. High-frequency yields speed and parallelism yields capacity. This sounds good if there is adequate room in the electromagnetic spectrum for a high-frequency wide-band signal.

Classical radio and TV signals operate in the 50 MHz to 1.0 GHz range, or in terms of wavelength, carrier wave peaks are up to 30 cm (11.8 in.) apart. The frequency of visible light is many orders of magnitude higher at 400–770 THz—peaks are one-millionth of an inch apart. Each country has rules governing its own allocation of spectrum to 5G, but they all restrict 5G signals to somewhere below visible light and somewhere above TV and radio, say one to several hundred GHz, which means a typical wave is less than a US postage stamp wide. This is important because an antenna must be long enough to capture at least 1/2 of a wavelength. So, the first feature of 5G signaling is the ability to transmit and receive signals from small antennas. This is often called *mmwave* signaling, because mm stands for millimeter size. Postage-stamp-sized antennas also fit nicely inside the small form factor of a smart phone.

Small antennas for transmission and capture of high-frequency signals have their price, however, because high-frequency signals require more power to reach the same distance. And more power means more battery capacity, which is at odds with mobile computing. In addition, mmwaves travel in straight line of sight, which limits their range to about one kilometer, and they bounce off of buildings, which produces ghost signals. To overcome these obstacles, communication engineers have devised extremely clever designs and algorithms. Basically, they invented 128 ears to listen to very faint signals.

MASSIVELY MIMO

MIMO (Multiple Input, Multiple Output) means exactly what it says—devices receive many inputs and send many outputs at the same time. In a massive MIMO system, many antennas are used in concert to focus the energy into a directed beam facing the source of the signal or its target destination, plus algorithms for listening harder in one direction than another.

A typical 5G device will have from 64 to 256 antennas and sophisticated algorithms for consolidation of multiple echoes (signals bouncing off buildings) to focus energy in the direction of source or destination. The six-sided hexagonal design of cellular towers from Bell Labs will no longer do. MIMO requires more than six surfaces to focus signals and fend off interference from ghosts and other signals. Antenna design becomes a new art in the era of 5G.

In 2018, Qualcomm announced the first mmwave antenna for 5G smart phones—the QTM052—containing 16 antennas in 2×2 mmwave arrays

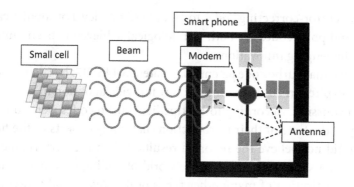

FIGURE 8.1 A typical 5G smart phone connects to an Internet service provider via a small cell tuned to licensed MIMO frequencies.

each located along one of the four edges of the device, and then connected to an X50 modem (modulator/demodulator) the size of a penny. See Figure 8.1. When combined with software, the 16 antennas work in concert to focus the arrays on the source or destination such that signal strength is maximized. The rest is software.

A gross simplification is that MIMO plus QAM at mm wavelength equals 5G. With 128 or more QAM channels operating at 10 GHz and low latency, it is feasible to accommodate 100× more devices than currently connected to the Internet via wireless and wired links.

But higher frequencies means shorter ranges. The 5G signal cannot travel very far without consuming too much battery power. So, 5G needs a much more dense array of ground stations—what developers call *small cells*, so that 5G devices are never more than one kilometer away from an access point. This build-out may slow proliferation of 5G, but over time, 5G networks will replace Wi-Fi for short communications and cellular for long distances. But, we still need to turbocharge the signal.

TURBO-CHARGING THE SIGNAL

Clever engineering is still not enough to pick out a signal from weak and noisy backgrounds, so even stronger error detection and correction algorithm is needed. The Turbo code was briefly described earlier.* It has been used since 3G was introduced a decade ago, but it is even more essential now because 5G signals are typically weaker and buried in more noise. Turbo codes arrived just in time. The concept underlying Turbo coding

---

* Berrou C. and A. Glavieux (1996). Near Optimum Error Correcting Coding and Decoding: Turbo-Codes. *IEEE Transactions on Communications*, 44(10), pp. 1261–1271.

has taken error-correcting codes to an even higher level of sophistication. Turbo and polar codes are both technological achievements and intellectually challenging innovations.

The original Turbo code patent (U.S. Patent 5,446,747) by Claude Berrou (1973–) expired in 2013 opening the way for wide adoption in cellular signal transmission. According to Wikipedia, "Turbo codes were so revolutionary at the time of their introduction that many experts in the field of coding did not believe the reported results. When the performance was confirmed a small revolution in the world of coding took place that led to the investigation of many other types of iterative signal processing."* Turbo codes come close to the Shannon information theory ideal without being overly complex encoding and decoding algorithms. [However, the computational load is greater than with other codes.] The greater signal carrying capacity of 5G further opens the door to more redundancy and better error-correction algorithms.

The Turbo code algorithm has been compared with finding the solution to a crossword puzzle where a letter is missing. For example, in a crossword puzzle vertical letters might spell C?W and horizontal letters H?RSE. The objective is to find the missing letter at the "?" intersection to correctly spell COW and HORSE. In this simple example, the obvious answer is the letter O, but in a more elaborate crossword puzzle, discovery may depend on the clues provided by the game. These clues are like evidence in solving a mystery. They bring us closer to the truth, or what is believed to be the truth, until we eventually confirm the truth.

Turbo coding is more sophisticated than a crossword puzzle, however, it is still a kind of guessing game whereby clues are provided by decoders that decide if a noisy bit is zero or one, along with estimates of their confidence in the answer backed by evidence. A typical Turbo code uses two encoder/decoder algorithms—let us call one *vertical* and the other *horizontal* to continue the crossword puzzle analog. The original message is encoded twice—once by the vertical encoder and again by the horizontal encoder. The original message and its two encodings are transmitted to a receiver where information gleaned from all three "copies" of the message is used to decode the original message. [Note: this "extreme redundancy" is a drawback, but 5G can afford it.]

Suppose the vertical algorithm computes parity checking bits on the original message and the horizontal algorithm computes parity bits on a

---

* https://en.wikipedia.org/wiki/Turbo_code

permuted or scrambled copy of the original message. Scrambling the order of bits or symbols is called *interleaving*—it simply shuffles the order like shuffling a deck of poker playing cards. The idea here is that a burst of noise that obfuscates, say, the first three information bits, is unlikely to obfuscate the same bits if they are in different positions in the interleaved sequence. By performing two encodings of the same information but in different order, the decoders gather evidence just like gathering clues in a crossword puzzle.

It is assumed there are errors in the signal when the three copies are received. So the task of decoding must exploit the redundancy as well as the unlikely chance that an error in the vertical decoder also appears in the horizontal decoder. A Turbo code uses the results of the vertical decoder to check on and improve on the results of the horizontal decoder. Initially, the decoder assumes error bits are just as likely as correct bits. The vertical decoder computes a *soft output*, which is an estimate of the correct bit value, based on voltages obtained from the signal. [We assume voltages range from −1.0 representing a zero bit and +1.0 for a one bit. They can also be any value in between due to noise.] The soft outputs from vertical are passed to the horizontal decoder, and the soft output from the horizontal decoder are passed to the vertical decoder, etc. This back-and-forth iterative process is repeated several times, typically not more than 10–15 times.

Iteration improves on the probability that a voltage in [−1.0 to +1.0] correctly represents a binary [0, 1] digit.

Turbo codes consume more computation and are highly redundant so it is clear they are less efficient in terms of bandwidth utilization, but more efficient in terms of channel capacity because they enhance signal-to-noise ratio, S/N. "Excessive redundancy" was a disadvantage in earlier years, but now computation is fast and cheap so Turbo coding in addition to QAM is able to exploit the "excessive redundancy."

Turbo codes are a new breed of encoder/decoder that harkens all the way back to the beginning in the 1970s. This new breed finds the "true value" of a bit based on a belief network rather than an algebraic formula. Thus, Turbo codes are a departure from earlier generations of error-correcting codes.

CODES AS BELIEF NETWORKS

Error-correcting codes have evolved from Hamming code to Turbo codes over a span of more than 50 years. They appear to be different approaches to the same problem—detecting and correcting information in a noisy channel. Recently, however, it has become apparent that they all have one thing in common: they are special cases of *belief propagation systems* based on Bayesian belief networks. Bayesian networks rely on conditional probability rather than algebraic coding as in cyclic GF(2) codes. Belief is defined as a conditional probability such as:

$$\Pr\left(A \text{ and } B\right) = \Pr\left(A\right) \Pr\left(B \text{ given } A\right)$$

In plain English this says, "The likelihood that both A and B are true is the product of the likelihood of A and the conditional probability that B is true when we know A is true." Bayes avoided the notion of a probability and instead called it a belief. Hence a Bayesian network is a network of events that increase or decrease beliefs due to the collection of evidence in the form of Pr(A) and Pr(B given A).

A code word containing unreliable bits (voltages) can be thought of as representing the probability the bit is correct. In turn, the probability that a bit is correct is called a *belief* in a belief propagation system. If the probability is 1.0, we believe the bit is correct. If it is zero, we believe the bit is incorrect. Fractions between zero and one represent a level of belief that the bit is correct.

The probability of a bit's correctness is a measure of belief obtained by collecting evidence.

Redundancy is exploited in various ways by encoding/decoding algorithms that turn evidence into a belief, ranging from zero to one. Actually, if we believe a bit is incorrect, we know that it is correct if flipped. Checking bits can also be incorrect due to noise, so it is not sufficient to place complete confidence in checking bits. Error-correcting codes must check the checking bits, too. By collecting evidence from both information and checking bits, we can home in on the correct values. This is called *belief propagation*, BP, because algorithms collect evidence to incrementally build up (or down) the probability that a bit is correct. In the case of Hamming codes, parity bits provide an initial level of belief, and parity bits that check on other parity bits provide more belief. Turbo codes operate in a similar, but much more sophisticated, manner, to build up or propagate belief from one stage to another until the value of a bit is more certain to be correct than not.

A Turbo code is a type of BP algorithm.

BP algorithms tend to be shrouded in alien terminology. Pr(A) is called *a priori* probability, and Pr(A given B) is called *a posteriori* probability. Generally, the "a" is dropped so that Baye's theorem reads like the following:

$$\Pr\big(B \text{ given } A\big) = \Pr\big(A \text{ and } B\big)\big/\Pr\big(A\big)$$

Posteriori probability = new evidence/priori probability

The *posteriori* probability is obtained from new evidence Pr(A and B) and *priori* evidence Pr(A) to get the MAP (Maximum *a posteriori*) formulation of Turbo coding:

Level of Belief = new evidence/existing evidence

Iteration of the vertical and horizontal decoder algorithms produces enhanced "new evidence" from previous "existing evidence." The "level of belief" either increases or decreases, depending of subsequent "new evidence." After many iterations, Pr(A and B) ceases to change, which indicates it has reached a maximum value, hence the designation *MAP*.

Actually, any type of vertical and horizontal algorithm can be used as long as they are interleaved so that one coding scheme checks on the other and iterations improve on one another. This idea has stimulated a long series of innovations in the evolution of Turbo codes. It is why there is more than one Turbo code. Each successive generation improves on earlier generations. In fact, self-correcting and iterative algorithms for error detection and correction might all be considered early versions of BP algorithms.

Coding theorist pioneer Robert McEliece (1942–) et al. says,

> One of the most interesting historical aspects of the turbo decoding problem is how often in the past inventors of decoding algorithms have hit upon a BP-like algorithm... With hindsight it is now evident that [earlier] algorithms can be viewed as a kind of belief propagation.*

In 1998, he predicted that BP-like algorithms would eventually be shown to be near optimal decoders largely because of the "pseudorandom interleaver ensuring that the resulting overall code behaves very much like

---

* McEliece, Robert J., David J. C. MacKay, and Jung-Fu Cheng (Feb. 1998). Turbo Decoding as an Instance of Pearl's "Belief Propagation" Algorithm. *IEEE J. Selected Areas in Communication*, 16(2), pp. 140–152.

a long random code, and by Shannon's theorems, a long random code is likely to be good in the sense of having the potential, with optimal decoding, to achieve performance near channel capacity."

By the twenty-first century, coding theory experts like McEliece realized the progressively more sophisticated algorithms were based on the same fundamental mathematical foundation—they are versions of Hidden Markov Models (HMM). The word "hidden" is significant, because the "real underlying process" is hidden from direct observation and measurement. The trick is to discover the hidden underlying process by experimentation and measurement. The measurements, as it turns out, are Bayesian beliefs, so the *Viterbi algorithm*, for example, is a simple Bayesian belief network formulated as a Hidden Markov Model.

Error correction by successive estimation of the likelihood that a symbol is correct is a Bayesian belief network process based on a Hidden Markov Model. Forney was one of the earliest pioneers to realize that the Viterbi algorithm—and subsequent algorithms that refined the Viterbi algorithm—are Bayesian networks, and that the unwinding of a Bayesian network in time can be represented in a *Trellis diagram*. Forney's observation greatly simplified the complicated terminology and entangled concepts emerging from over 40 years of innovation.

Figure 8.2 illustrates the Viterbi–Forney concept of MAP represented as a Trellis diagram. The name comes from the garden variety of trellis used to prop up rose bushes. The objective is to decide if a signal containing voltages or frequencies that encode a zero as −1 and a one as +1 are received correctly, and if not, to correct them. The signal is noisy so it is initially not clear whether the receiver is receiving a plus or minus one. Therefore, starting at initial state START in Figure 8.2, the algorithm

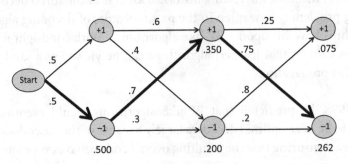

FIGURE 8.2 A typical Trellis diagram traces the unwinding of a Markov model over time as evidence is gathered at each time step. The MAP path is the maximum likelihood path along bold states and transitions.

assumes each occur equally likely. The experiment transitions to either +1 or −1 with probability 0.500.

Additional experiments produce additional soft outputs and posteriori estimates of the likelihood that the symbol is a +1 or −1. The next stage reading from left to right in Figure 8.2 produces transition probabilities that the symbol is +1 or −1 as shown. The final stage produces final posteriori estimates such that the maximum likelihood probability of +1 is 0.075, and the maximum probability of −1 is 0.262. Therefore, the voltage is −1, because 0.262 is greater than 0.075.

The Viterbi path working backward from 0.262 to 0.350, 0.500, and eventually START yields MAP—the Maximum a posteriori answer. In this example, the symbol is a zero, because the Viterbi path ends with state −1. This algorithm is often called SOVA—Soft Output Viterbi Algorithm. SOVA is an example of a more general BP-like code.

McEliece and Forney were not only correct in observing that earlier codes are special cases of the more general BP-like codes, but future codes will be even more general versions of BP-like codes. Forney's Trellis diagram is a common tool used to visualize these codes. Further note that the optimal Viterbi path is also obtainable by dynamic programming, because it is simply the maximum likelihood path working backward as shown in Figure 8.2.

Modern error-correction codes are instances of Hidden Markov Models, typically represented by a Trellis diagram that reveals the Viterbi path, which is the Maximum a posteriori (MAP) solution.

POLAR CODES

If two encoder/decoder algorithms come close to the Shannon limit, and computational power is no barrier to practical application, then four encoder/decoder algorithms should come even closer to the Shannon limit. And eight encoder/decoder algorithms should be even better, etc. Where does it end?

In the 1990s, BP-like codes required too much computation to be practical, but by 2013 when the Turbo code patent expired, adequate computational power fit in the palm of a consumer's hand. The BP-like Turbo code became practical and because 5G signals operate over weak noisy channels, it became essential. But in 2009, Turkish scientist Erdal Arikan (1958–) generalized the BP-like Turbo code even further. His idea is both simple and messy. Luckily, modern computers can handle messy.

Arikan's *polar code* derives its name from the concept of polarization— separation of messages into sharply contrasting sets. Arikan's polar code extends simple separation illustrated by the Turbo code vertical/horizontal algorithm into multiple separations or poles. A polar code uses all available channels of a 5G signal to redundantly encode and decode noisy signals. Think of the polar code as a Turbo code on steroids.

Encoding combines the original message with interleaved or randomly permutated copies into pairs, then pairs into 4-tuples, 4-tuples into 8-tuples, etc., up to some reasonable limit. Each "interleaved" copy is a different permutation of the original message so belief propagation from one copy to the other can be performed during decoding. This is ideal for 5G with 128 ears, because polar codes can use all 128 channels for scrambling copies of the original message. The multiple scrambled copies are transmitted over separate channels of a multi-channel QAM (Quadrature Amplitude Modulation) communication system typical of 5G, where they are likely to encounter noise.

Instead of iterating between vertical and horizontal decoders as in a Turbo code, the polar code algorithm applies BP-like belief calculations to select channels more likely to contain the correct information bits. Since channels contain permutated copies of the encoded message, Maximum a posteriori (MAP) selection tends to select the channel with the correct bits. The information in the "successful" channels is "believed" and the others ignored. According to Arikan, polar coding sends data only through channels with high probability of containing correct bits.* Obviously, accuracy improves as more channels are used so that back-and-forth iterating between vertical and horizontal algorithms is not needed.

Polar codes are as redundant as the transmission channel allows. If 64 channels of QAM are available, the polar code can apply MAP to 64 copies. If 128 channels are available, it can apply MAP to 128 copies. As the number of channels approaches infinity, the Shannon limit approaches perfection. Sending multiple copies of the message through a serial channel decreases bandwidth, but if there are as many QAM channels as copies, the net result is as if one copy is sent through one channel.

Polar codes may be a temporary solution to Shannon perfection as other factors such as power and suppression of ghost signals raise the bar and force communications engineers to devise even more ingenious algorithms. Meanwhile, Turbo and polar codes are staples of 5G.

---

* Arikan, Erdal (July 2009). Channel Polarization: A Method for Constructing Capacity-Achieving Codes for Symmetric Binary-Input Memoryless Channels. *IEEE Trans. Inform. Theory*, 55, pp. 3051–3073.

COMMENT

The signal and corresponding error-correcting schemes to encode/decode it have matured from complicated and ingenious algorithms to brute-force and computationally intense algorithms. Hamming and Reed–Solomon codes based on Galois field theory are exotic and highly mathematical. Turbo and polar codes are also rooted in deep mathematics, but also computationally intense. After all, they are based on "extreme redundancy"—many permutations checking each other—and the simplicity of Baye's theorem for accumulating evidence of correctness. Reducing them to Markov models and Trellis diagrams does not reduce the amount of computation required.

Simplicity has shifted the burden onto faster and cheaper hardware and software that is able to process redundant copies of the signal in real-time. This feat was not possible a decade ago. But it is now, or at least until the requirements for communication speed and efficiency takes another leap from gigahertz to terahertz and beyond. Then what? Will the rift in computing exploited by Gary Kildall and Bill Gates repeat with a new generation of communications innovators? What is the limit?

CHAPTER 9

Spooky Action at a Distance

HEINRICH AND HELMUT ARE identical twins. When standing next to one another, even their parents cannot tell them apart. They both part their dark brown hair on the right side and they sound alike when speaking. One might draw the wrong conclusion, however, about what they are thinking at any instant in time, because they are contrarians. Whatever Heinrich wants, Helmut rejects; whatever Helmut thinks, Heinrich thinks the opposite, and vice versa.

When they were growing up, Helmut wanted a red wagon, but Heinrich did not. Heinrich played soccer but Helmut hated the sport. If Heinrich said the sun is shining, Helmut would automatically say it was not. Whatever one twin is doing the other twin is likely doing the exact opposite. Their thoughts are negatively correlated such that when Heinrich says something is "up," Helmut always says it is "down."

A statistician might say the thinking of the twins is negatively correlated or entangled. But the Heinrich–Helmut entanglement is extreme— the correlation coefficient is always minus one, and nothing in between. When one twin says heads the other says tails so the expected value of tossing a coin is always "coins differ." If heads is +1 and tails is −1, then the correlation is always $+1(-1) = -1$, for the two brothers. They are mathematically pure opposites.

Friends of the twins are never sure what Heinrich and Helmut are thinking, but they are sure that the thoughts of one twin are connected with the thoughts of the other twin in a contrarian way. Ask Heinrich to predict the outcome of a tossed coin, and his answer is always the opposite of Helmut's answer. This provided ample fun for friends of the twins, who made up a coin-tossing parlor game to amuse themselves. The friends blindfolded and placed the twins in separate rooms and then asked each to predict whether a tossed coin is heads or tails. The twins are isolated from one another so they cannot see or hear one another. Nonetheless, if Heinrich predicts "heads," Helmut predicts "tails," and vice versa. Mathematically, the two predictions always produce a correlated answer of $+1(-1) = -1$.

Nobody has figured out how the twins do it. One theory is that the two are telepathic. They are said to be in a state of *superposition* before guessing the result of a tossed coin. Superposition means a tossed coin is heads up and tails up at the same time in the twin's minds. That is, both Heinrich and Helmut think the tossed coin is simultaneously heads up and tails up until they blurt out a decision. When one twin declares the coin is heads, the other twin simultaneously declares the opposite.

In superposition, both outcomes are possible and equally likely, so the combined Heinrich–Helmut state is heads *and* tails until one of the twins calls out his prediction. Neither twin is willing to speculate until the coin is actually tossed and a measurement taken. The instant that Heinrich, for example, declares the coin to be heads up, the superposition state of the combined twins *collapses*, and Heinrich "knows" the coin is heads up and Helmut "knows" the coin is tails up. Somehow each twin "feels" the other's decision. When the superposition state no longer exists, friends observe the contrary decisions of the twins at the same time, thus wiping out uncertainty.

The twins and their friends continued to play this game throughout adulthood. Only they made it more sophisticated by moving the twins further and further apart. Unsurprisingly, they still give contrarian answers to the coin-tossing game when Heinrich is in Paris and Helmut is in Los Angeles. In fact, they give contrarian answers regardless of how far apart they are. Even spookier is the observation that there is no elapsed time between Heinrich's decision in Paris and Helmut's decision in Los Angeles. Light takes .03 seconds to travel from Paris to Los Angeles, and yet the elapsed time between decisions is zero. Apparently, clairvoyant thought travels faster than the speed of light.

The mental states of Heinrich and Helmut are somehow *entangled*. Before deciding whether a tossed coin is going to turn up heads or tails, the twins are in a superposition state whereby the outcome is both heads and tails. This means both states exist at the same time with equal probability. Heinrich may declare heads or tails with equal probability and similarly Helmut may declare heads or tails with equal probability. Friends simply do not know which twin might decide first, nor what decision a twin will make, until a decision by either twin is made public. When the public decision is announced, superposition collapses and there is no longer any uncertainty regarding the answer. If Heinrich says heads, it is certain that Helmut will say tails.

The mystery is this: regardless of how far apart Heinrich and Helmut are from one another, a decision by one instantaneously determines the contrary decision by the other one. There is no time for cheating because there is no time delay between Heinrich's decision and Helmut's decision, and vice versa. The collapse of superposition propagates faster than the speed of light. How is this possible?

This unusual talent bothered Heinrich and Helmut so much they both became quantum physicists to find out why and how they were clairvoyant. Of course, Heinrich's theory was different than Helmut's. Helmut maintains he is right and Heinrich is wrong. Now with a Ph.D. in physics, Heinrich explains the instantaneous transmission of his decision to Helmut as an example of *hidden variables* in action. He claims that quantum physics lacks a complete explanation for how his clairvoyance actually works without throwing in some hidden variables.

According to Heinrich's theory, the identical twins are linked together by a combined state that cannot be separated out without disturbing both sub-states. Measuring a property of a combined state tweaks hidden variables causing the states to separate out and express themselves as contrary decisions. The hidden variables link *conjugate pairs* such as time/energy, position/momentum, spin up/down, etc. Measurement or observation causes superposition to collapse conjugate pairs so that one conjugate is "up" and the other is "down."

Helmut's theory is quite different, because Helmut always disagrees with Heinrich. When Heinrich married a blonde woman, Helmut married a brunette, of course. When Heinrich wears a blue suit, Helmut wears a brown suit. When Heinrich proposed a theory of entanglement through the actions of hidden variables hidden away out of sight, Helmut instantaneously proposed a contrary theory based on predeterminism. It goes as follows. Predictions made by one twin are predetermined extending backward in time through a light cone all the way back to the beginning of time. The twins have no free will to make a decision of heads or tails. Instead, the declaration of heads or tails was decided eons ago. It is not necessary to communicate information at the speed of light or any other speed because the decision has already been made. We don't need hidden variables!

According to Helmut's theory, declaration of heads or tails is not random or spontaneous at all. His decision, and therefore Heinrich's contrary decision, is made before the game begins. It is decided ahead of time, such that there is no need for information to travel faster than the speed of light or for conjugate pairs to be linked by hidden variables. Determinism has already provided friends with each twin's answer.

Which theory is correct? Helmut proposes a theory of determinism that most people reject because we like to think we exercise free will. We are not robots programmed from birth to act out a script that was written long before our time. It smacks of the Prime Mover idea proposed by Aristotle 2,300 years ago. On the other hand, Heinrich proposes a theory without predeterminism that is also difficult to accept because it sounds like magic and does not explain how an entangled system remains entangled over long distances. If Heinrich is right, the entangled state of Heinrich–Helmut remains coherent regardless of separation in time and space. Decisions were made even before Heinrich and Helmut were born.

Entanglement seems to be a paradox, because it either violates realism (non-determinism) or the speed of light. Or, it could simply be wrong because our understanding of physical laws is incomplete. Maybe there is a *loophole* in the coin-tossing game played by Helmut and Heinrich.

THE EPR PARADOX

In 1935, Albert Einstein (1879–1955), Boris Podolsky (1896–1966), and Nathan Rosen (1909–1995) published a paper in *Physical Review* titled, "Can Quantum Mechanical Description of Physical Reality Be Considered Complete?"[*] The paper describes a *Gedankenexperiment*—a thought experiment of the kind that Einstein was famous for. The thought experiment involves too much math to be described here, so I have simplified the argument considerably. But the reader should already know the answer, because it parallels the Heinrich–Helmut parable.

The EPR authors proposed a paradox as follows. Two particles A and B travel in opposite directions, perhaps after colliding head-on with one

---

[*] Einstein, A., B. Podolsky, and N. Rosen (1935). *Physics Review,* 47, p. 777.

another, until Helmut observes the position of A. With the exact value of A's position, we can calculate the exact position of B using classical laws handed down to us by Isaac Newton. Now, suppose Heinrich simultaneously measures the exact momentum of particle B. He uses B's momentum to calculate the exact momentum of particle A. Taken together, Helmut and Heinrich know the exact positions and momentum of particles A and B, but according to the Heisenberg Uncertainty Principle, it is impossible to know with certainty both position and momentum.

Either Heisenberg's Uncertainty Principle that says it is impossible to make exact measurements of conjugate pairs such as position and momentum is wrong, or information can travel faster than the speed of light. In the thought experiment, an imaginary particle is tracked through time according to Schrodinger's equation—the equation that describes the time-varying dynamics of a quantum level particle such as a photon. Measurement of the particle's location or momentum—a *conjugate pair* invokes the Heisenberg's Uncertainty Principle that says measuring position indirectly affects momentum and conversely, measuring momentum indirectly affects position. According to Heisenberg, there is a lower limit on measurements involving conjugate pairs like position and momentum. Increasing the precision of one lowers the precision of the other. Attempts to determine a quantum particle's exact location, reduces the exactness of its momentum.

By 1935, physicists were pretty sure that nothing can travel faster than the speed of light and Heisenberg's Uncertainty Principle was accepted as correct, experimentally. Conjugate pairs of measurable properties like time/energy and position/velocity obeyed the famous uncertainty principle. This was confirmed by experiments carried out by many skeptical researchers over a period of years following Heisenberg's claim. So, the EPR paradox was indeed a paradox, because it required Einstein and co-authors to either reject the speed-of-light limitation or the Heisenberg principle. The ERP team was loath to do either one.

The 1935 paper remains in the top 10 most impactful papers ever published in a *Physical Review* journal. The sophistication of quantum theory evolved quickly partially due to this paper. But, Einstein was not convinced of the validity of his own paper! Later he said, "It did not come out as well as I had originally wanted." It was Podolsky's idea, really, but it stimulated a half-century of debate, even though the answer was yes and no. Yes, quantum mechanics can answer the question, and no, quantum theory is not complete. Einstein sided with twin brother Heinrich, claiming that quantum mechanics lacks something. It is an incomplete formulation of physical reality because it cannot explain the instantaneous transmission of information required by entanglement without introducing hidden variables. He did not, however, suggest what those hidden variables are.

An entry in the Stanford Encyclopedia of Philosophy says,

> Initially Einstein was enthusiastic about the quantum theory. By 1935, however, while recognizing the theory's significant achievements, his enthusiasm had given way to disappointment. His reservations were twofold. Firstly, he felt the theory had abdicated the historical task of natural science to provide knowledge of significant aspects of nature that are independent of observers or their observations. Instead the fundamental understanding of the quantum wave function (alternatively, the "state function," "state vector," or "psi-function") was that it only treated the outcomes of measurements (via probabilities given by the Born Rule). The theory was simply silent about what, if anything was likely to be true in the absence of observation. That there could be laws, even probabilistic laws, for finding things if one looks, but no laws of any sort for how things are independently of whether one looks, marked quantum theory as irrealist. Secondly, the quantum theory was essentially statistical. The probabilities built into the state function were fundamental and, unlike the situation in classical statistical mechanics, they were not understood as arising from ignorance of fine details. In this sense the theory was indeterministic. Thus Einstein began to probe how strongly the quantum theory was tied to irrealism and indeterminism.*

So Einstein and colleagues faced the same paradox that puzzles friends of Heinrich and Helmut. If Einstein sided with Heinrich, he had to admit to incompleteness of quantum mechanics, which undermined the solid work of Heisenberg and Einstein, himself. If he sided with Helmut and accepted predeterminism, he was giving in to "irrealism," or the unthinkable concept of a Prime Mover and the elimination of free will. He did not like either choice, and rejected entanglement, altogether. Entanglement was not experimentally verified during his lifetime, so the paradox was shoved aside for the time being.

---

* https://plato.stanford.edu/entries/qt-epr/

If it existed, Einstein called entanglement "spooky action at a distance," because it violated his sense of realism and belief in the determinism of nature. It resonated with his claim that "God would not play dice" with the universe. His criticism started a rash of experiments that continue to confirm entanglement to this day. "Quantum entanglement has been demonstrated experimentally with photons, neutrinos, electrons, molecules as large as Bucky balls, and even small diamonds."* Einstein was wrong.

Erwin Schrodinger (1887–1961) coined the term *entanglement* after being dragged into the debate following publication of the EPR paper. After all, his 1925 equation was used in the thought experiment and was only ten years old. This is barely enough time to establish it as a foundation. Maybe Schrodinger felt insecure. Regardless, the term caught on and remains the term used to describe spooky action that remains largely a mystery, today.

Here is what the EPR paradox eventually established:

Two particles can become entangled such that when the state of a particular property is measured in one particle, the opposite state is observed on the entangled particle instantaneously. This is true regardless of the distance separating the entangled particles, so measuring the state of one particle instantaneously informs the other particle.

HEISENBERG'S SECRET (ADVANCED)

The Heisenberg uncertainty principle is often misunderstood. Most of us think the uncertainty stems from the belief that measuring something also disturbs it. But this is not an explanation for uncertainty. Rather, uncertainty only applies to conjugate pairs, because one conjugate pair property is a Fourier Transform of the other conjugate pair property. Momentum is the Fourier Transform of location, and location is the inverse Fourier Transform of momentum. Heisenberg's uncertainty principle only applies to conjugate pairs.

Suppose measurements are taken of location and momentum of a photon. We know that location is defined as a wave-like probability distribution rather than a single number. More precisely, location versus time is a wave-like solution to the Schrodinger equation. Since location and momentum are conjugates, momentum is the Fourier Transform of the location distribution. This is why they are called a conjugate pair. So, calculation of momentum is essentially a transformation of time-varying

---

* https://en.wikipedia.org/wiki/Quantum_entanglement

location waves into frequency varying power spectral density as described in Chapter 4.

Recall Figure 4.6 in Chapter 4 showing how the signal in the frequency domain spreads out and flattens as the signal in the time domain becomes shorter. A spike in time translates into a flat wave in the frequency domain. In terms of quantum mechanics, this says as measurement time becomes shorter, momentum (frequency) becomes flatter. In other words, as location measurements get more precise, momentum measurements become less precise, and the reverse.

$$\Delta x \cdot \Delta p \geq \frac{h}{2};$$

Where h is Planck's constant—a very small number.[*]

The product of location and momentum has a physical limit as particles scale downward. In fact, the limit is 1/2 Planck's constant, which in quantum theory is the smallest quantum of action possible in the physical world. Planck's constant bounds the product, because p shrinks as x grows, and x shrinks as p grows due to the Fourier Transform and its inverse. The Heisenberg Uncertainty Principle is a real-world limitation because of Planck's constant and the property of Fourier Transforms that connect conjugate pairs to one another. Reality obeys strict mathematical rules.

The Heisenberg uncertainty principle is a byproduct of mathematical models of reality at extremely small scales. Any conjugate pair of properties such as location and momentum is Fourier Transforms of one another. The Fourier Transform of one conjugate is inversely proportional to the other conjugate with constant of proportionality equal to h/2.

SPOOKY ACTION REDUX

Perhaps the distraction of the Great Depression during the 1930s or the war during the 1940s was responsible for the giant pause between publication of the EPR paradox and enunciation of Bell's theorem in the 1960s. Maybe Einstein was simply 30 years ahead of his time. For whatever reason, the EPR paradox and the implication that a spooky action actually takes place at the quantum level remained idle curiosity until John Stewart Bell (1928–1990) appeared on the scene. An Irishman married to another

---

[*] $6.62607015 \times 10^{-34}$ Joule-seconds.

noted physicist, Bell's day job was studying particle physics, but his hobby was quantum physics. He was especially intrigued by the EPR paradox.

In 1964, Bell wrote a paper titled, "On the Einstein-Podolsky-Rosen Paradox"* and breathed life back into the speculation that entanglement is real. Bell's theorem says, "No physical theory of local hidden variables can ever produce all of the predictions of quantum mechanics."† The EPR paradox came alive once again following *Bell's theorem*.

The alternative to the hidden variables theory is either a belief in predeterminism or repeal of the speed of light limit. In 1985 Bell said,

> There is a way to escape the inference of superluminal speeds and spooky action at a distance. But it involves absolute determinism in the universe, the complete absence of free will. There is no need for a faster-than-light signal to tell particle A what measurement has been carried out on particle B, because the universe, including particle A, already "knows" what that measurement, and its outcome, will be.

Bell opened the unhealed wound of quantum mechanics that had been smoothed over for decades. Because of Bell, researchers renewed their search for a resolution to the paradox. Eventually, a theory of quantum entanglement would answer the paradox without violating the speed of light limitation or introducing irrealism—an explanation that Einstein rejected. A hint to the suffering reader: photons travel at the speed of light, which consumes time. As a system, entangled photons must carry their superposition state with them on their 9,100-mile 0.03 second journey from Paris to Los Angeles. This delay must be included in any analysis of the EPR paradox. Specifically, any signal carried by photons 9,100 miles apart cannot travel faster than the photons, themselves.

Meanwhile, science-fiction writers have had a field day with entanglement operating instantaneously over long distances. Action at a distance became fashionable following experiments that verified entanglement.

ATTACK OF THE SOPHONS FROM TRISOLARA

Liu Cixin (1963–) wrote the most popular science-fiction novel in China in 2007, and won the Hugo Award for Best Novel in 2015 for *The Three Body*

---

* Bell, J.S. (1964). *Physics*, 1, p. 195.
† https://en.wikipedia.org/wiki/Bell%27s_theorem

Problem—an epic story stretching 450 years into the future. It gained a substantial foothold in America after President Obama declared it a useful distraction from his problems with Congress. At the time this was written, Amazon.com was in talks to commit nearly $1 billion to a TV version of the novel.

The central plot of Cixin's novel is an impending attack by an alien race 4.8 light years away. Unfortunately, the aliens live on a planet whiplashed by three suns that alternately scorch and freeze their planet as it plows a chaotic path around the three suns. Earthlings call the aliens Trisolarans because they come from a solar system with three suns—hence the name of the novel. The Trisolarans realize they have to abandon their three-body solar system or oscillate between two bad alternatives, forever. The book subsequently expanded into three books called the *Remembrance of Earth's Past* trilogy.

Traveling at one percent light speed, the alien Trisolarans take 450 years to arrive. This gives humans time to prepare. Meanwhile, they have planted *sophons* on earth to spy on earthlings and turn some fearful people into traitors. Communication between Earth and Trisolaran leaders is done through the planted sophons—a faster-than-light-speed communication channel that works instantaneously because of entangled photons. The success of the Trisolaran migration—and the novel's plot—depends on entanglement.

Cixin uses spooky action at a distance so his characters can communicate across the vastness of space. A measurement performed on a photon on the Trisolaran planet is instantaneously entangled with a photon on Earth. Information bits are encoded as conjugate pairs of photons sharing a property such as spin up/down or polarization left/right. Instantaneous communication across 4.8 light years of space is spooky action.

The same idea has captured the attention of serious scientists working in China and elsewhere. Pan Jian-Wei (1970–), at the University of Science and Technology in Shanghai, demonstrated a type of sophon communication in 2016 when the 600-kg Micius satellite beamed entangled photons to mountain tops on Earth separated by 1,200 km, setting a new distance record for entanglement.* One photon (Helmut) is entangled with another photon (Heinrich) 1,200 km away.

---

* Popkin, Gabriel (2017). China's Quantum Satellite Achieves "spooky action" at a Record Distance. *Science* (Jun 15, 2017). https://www.sciencemag.org/news/2017/06/china-s-quantum-satellite-achieves-spooky-action-record-distance

The scientists aimed a laser at a crystal containing correlated photons and then transported one reflected photon to a ground station in Tibet and the other reflected photon to a ground station in Austria. For example, a Blu-ray laser can split correlated photons into two, measure the pair's properties, and send them via laser to anywhere on earth—all from onboard a satellite. The apparatus fits on a 10 cm by 10 cm printed circuit board and is rugged enough to survive the g-forces of rocket launch.*

Another hint: how long did it take for the Pan Jian-Wei team to transmit the entangled photons to separate locations 1,200 km apart? Hint, hint: it didn't happen instantaneously.

While quantum communication across long distances on earth has only recently been demonstrated, the idea of using entanglement to secure the signal goes back to the 1980s—long before the technology existed to make it work. Nearly forty years later, entanglement is being applied almost daily to secure the signal. It has opened up an entirely new discipline called *Quantum Cryptography* (QC). This is where our story of the evolving signal continues.

THE KEY DISTRIBUTION PROBLEM

In the modern world of open systems and global connectivity, self-correcting signals are not enough. Signal transmission must be secure. Unfortunately, computer security has been under attack for decades without a surefire solution until now. Cryptography is an arms race with strong encryption methods being cracked by strong attacks followed by even stronger encryption that is eventually cracked by even stronger attacks. Both sides escalate the sophistication of their technology, mainly because processing power improves exponentially, and partly because of ever more clever algorithms.

Headline news is awash with stories about security breaches affecting millions of Internet users. It is a privacy and security epidemic. Why is cryptography so difficult? The first problem addressed by the pioneers of modern cryptography is called the problem of *key exchange*. Before Bob can encrypt and send a message to Alice, he must obtain a key used to obfuscate his message. But, how does Bob securely obtain the key? If he uses the same key too often, it will eventually be cracked, and if he frequently obtains a new key he risks interception and exposure of his key by man-in-the-middle hackers. Key distribution over the Internet must be at least as secure as encryption, itself. But, isn't this a circular conundrum? To get a secret key, Bob needs a secret key!

---

* https://phys.org/news/2016-06-quantum-satellite-device-technology-global.html#jCp

The key distribution problem was solved in 1976 by a team of Stanford University and University of California at Berkeley researchers led by Martin Hellman (1945–), his student Whitfield Diffie (1944–), and colleague Ralph Merkle (1952–). The Diffie–Hellman–Merkle Public Key distribution Infrastructure (PKI) has been the basis of secure Internet transmission since it became a standard in 1999 (called the IEEE X.509 standard).* It ingeniously distributes two separate keys to Internet users: a public key that anyone can use to encrypt signals sent to you, and a private key for decoding received signals that only you know and use. By separating the encryption key into two keys and always keeping one secret and always exposing the other key to the world, Diffie–Hellman–Merkle showed us how to safely distribute keys.

Almost immediately after the Diffie–Hellman–Merkle public–private key concept was published, three other brilliant computer scientists, Ron Rivest (1947–), Adi Shamir (1952–), and Leonard Adleman (1945–) published an algorithm that implements the Diffie–Hellman–Merkle concept using properties of prime numbers. The RSA algorithm soon became the RSA Corporation for producing and managing public–private keys. It depends on a generous supply of prime numbers. This requirement is its Achilles heel. I will describe this weakness more, later.

Let us see how Bob and Alice use the RSA algorithm to secure signals transmitted to one another. Bob and Alice create their private and public keys in the same way, so we only need to show how Bob does it—Alice does the same. Bob first selects two *secret* prime numbers, say P and Q, and another number D, which he uses to produce his private key. He multiplies P × Q to get a modulus, N, and then uses the following formula to decode encrypted messages sent to him.

Decode(m) = m^D **mod**(N); where **mod** means "remainder after division by N."

For example, let P = 5, Q = 11, N = 55, and D = 27, so Bob's private key is [27, 55]. Suppose Bob receives secret signal containing m = 6, what is the plain text corresponding to m?

Decode(6) = 6^{27} **mod**(55) = 41; after a lot of multiplication and modular division.

---

* Diffie, Whitfield and Martin Hellman (1976). New Directions in Cryptography. *IEEE Transactions on Information Theory*, 22(6), p. 644. doi:10.1109/TIT.1976.1055638.

Bob hides N = 55 and D = 27 as his private key and only uses it to decode messages sent to him. But other people, such as Alice, must encrypt messages to Bob using his public key. Bob must tell the world what his public key is. Suppose he uses the same N = 55 to produce a public key that everyone in the world can use to send him secret signals. Encrypting signals sent to Bob must follow the rule:

$$\text{Encode}(m) = m^E \bmod(55);$$

E must satisfy $E \times D = k(P - 1)(Q - 1) + 1$, for some $k > 1$. For example, E = 3 works. So, Bob's public key is [3, 55]. Alice uses Bob's public key to encrypt signal "41" as follows:

$$\text{Encode}(41) = 41^3 \bmod(55) = 6.$$

Bob uses his private key to decode "6" back into plain text "41." In this way, no one besides Bob knows his private key. As long as Alice uses Bob's public key to encode messages to Bob, and he uses his private key to decode messages from Alice, the system works without exposing to much key information to the outside world. The public–private key distribution scheme is secure because Bob never has to expose his private key to anyone else.

Alice does the same thing—she combines two prime numbers and an added number D to build her own private key, and uses the process just described to generate a public key known to the outside world. Bob uses her public key to encrypt messages sent to her, and Alice uses her private key to decrypt all messages sent to her. Everyone is safe and secure.

Or, are they?

By separating the two keys, the asymmetric Diffie–Hellman–Merkle algorithm makes it very difficult to invade Bob and Alice's privacy. A prying hacker must discover the secret P and Q prime numbers that underlie Bob and Alice's public–private key pair. Is this possible? Unfortunately, it is. Suppose a computer can find the prime factors of N in one microsecond. How many microseconds does it take to factor a ten-digit N? How long to crack a million-digit N? As computers get faster, the number of digits in N must get larger to fend off ever more powerful attacks. Currently, N must contain more than 256 bits to be considered "strong," and this number is doubling about as fast as Moore's law.

In fact, in 1994 Peter Shor (1959–) proposed using quantum computers to quickly factor large modulus N into prime factors P and Q by minimizing the difference, (N–PQ), using qubits. An experimental quantum computer successfully factored N = 56,153 into P = 233, Q = 241 in 2014. If Shor's algorithm scales to very large numbers, Diffie–Hellman–Merkle codes will be crackable almost instantaneously. This is big problem number one.

Problem number two for Diffie–Hellman–Merkle is the growing shortage of prime numbers. As far as we know, there are an infinite number of prime numbers if an infinite number of digits are allowed. Practically speaking, there is only a finite supply of prime numbers. With billions of public–private key pairs being used every day to support secure transactions over the global Internet, the finite number of primes is quickly used up. When a prime number has been used too often, it becomes a target for brute-force methods of discovery.

Problem number three comes down to users—keys are often protected by passwords that are far less secure than the keys, themselves, but once cracked, weak passwords can undermine even the strongest encryption scheme. Public–private key information is only as secure as the passwords used to protect them. In most cases, this is inadequate.

In other words, the 40-year foundation of Internet security is being slowly and surely wiped out as computers become more powerful and billions of prime numbers are being over-used or abused to construct public–private keys. The Diffie–Hellman–Merkle infrastructure is likely to come to the end of its utility in the next decade. But, there may be a solution:

Spooky action, or entanglement as Schrodinger called it, provides an opportunity to improve signal security by making the signal tamper-proof.

HEINRICH AND HELMUT, SECRET AGENTS

Quantum entanglement may be the answer, because it does not rely on prime numbers and there are no public–private keys! Quantum cryptography sidesteps the limitations of Diffie–Hellman–Merkle through the application of entanglement to computer security. Perhaps twin brothers Heinrich and Helmut can become couriers of secret messages, using their powers of entanglement!

Charles Bennett (1943–) and Gilles Brassard (1955–) proposed the first quantum cryptography protocol in 1984, which was subsequently proven to be secure, but clunky. Bennett quickly improved BB84, which led to BB92 being published in 1992. A series of improvements followed in 1999, 2003, 2004, 2009, 2012, and 2013. The big breakthrough came in 1991, however, when Artur Ekert (1961–) used entanglement as the basis of key distribution. Ekert's method—abbreviated E91—does not need prime numbers, but it needs entanglement.

Heinrich and Helmut may be thought of metaphorically, as a communication channel for passing secret signals back and forth in quantum time. Recall that Heinrich and Helmut are contrarians such that if Heinrich sends a "0" to Helmut, Helmut will observe a "1," and vice versa. This assumes there are no errors or tampering between Heinrich and Helmut. However, even quantum entanglement involves a certain level of error, so the solution must include an error-correction step. We can use one of the CRC codes described earlier, and augment the quantum channel with a classical digital channel that we use for error correction.

Suppose hacker Eve is a man-in-the-middle attempting to break into the Heinrich–Helmut channel. Further suppose Bob is in Paris with Heinrich and Alice is in Los Angeles with Helmut. By combining an error-correcting code such as the Reed–Solomon or any other CRC code in addition to entanglement, we can forget about prime numbers and the Diffie–Hellman–Merkle concept and deal directly with the signal as an entangled conjugate pair such as polarized photons, e.g., light. Since light can be polarized at multiple angles, a 90-degree filter can detect the binary equivalent of "0," and a 180-degree filter can detect a "1."

With Heinrich's assistance, Bob sends a quantum signal via a photon in Paris entangled with a photon in Los Angeles to Alice and Helmut. Alice and Helmut instantly observe the collapsed superposition of the entangled photons as a "0" or "1." Assuming there is no tampering by Eve, the plain text signal is "1" or "0," because Helmut is a contrarian. On the other hand, Alice cannot trust either "1" or "0" if Eve tampered with the signal in transit. Suspicious of all things involving security, Alice has to assume the signal may be in error. This is where the error-correcting encoding comes in. As described in previous chapters, a burst-mode error-correction code, such as the Reed–Solomon code, will detect and correct errors that may have been introduced by Eve or by Mother Nature as noise.

In one scheme for detecting tampering, Bob and Alice use an ordinary digital channel to exchange polarization information without exposing the bit stream as containing a "0" or "1." Instead, Alice reports back to Bob the polarization value—up or down, say, without reporting the value of each encoded photon. Bob compares his polarization values with Alice's list to decide if the signal has been tampered with. If it has been tampered with by Eve, the polarization values will not match. In this case, Bob transmits the message again, and the process is repeated. By comparing polarizations without values, the message can be validated.

Note that entangled photon pairs must be sent to Paris and Los Angeles at subluminal speed, hence communication does not violate light's speed limit. Also note that there is some back-and-forth confirmation between Bob and Alice that is also subject to the limitation of light speed. Sophons cannot exceed the speed of light after all, because of this housekeeping! Quantum mechanics is not incomplete after all and entanglement is not a paradox when the whole system is analyzed in terms of realism. And, because the quantum state is what is measured, and not the physical objects themselves, the instantaneous behavior of correlated conjugate photons does not violate relativistic physics. Einstein would approve.

Writing in *Nature* in 2012, John Matson summarizes the current state-of-the-art of quantum communication,

> Say Alice wants to teleport the quantum state of a photon to Bob. First she takes one member of a pair of entangled photons, and Bob takes the other. Then Alice lets her entangled photon interfere with the photon to be teleported and performs a polarization measurement whose outcome depends on the quantum state of both of her particles.
>
> Because of the link between Alice and Bob forged by entanglement, Bob's photon instantly feels the effect of the measurement made by Alice. Bob's photon assumes the quantum state of Alice's original photon, but in a sort of garbled form. Bob cannot recover the quantum state Alice wanted to teleport until he reverses that garbling by tweaking his photon in a way that depends on the outcome of Alice's measurement. So he must await word from Alice about how to complete the teleportation—and that word cannot travel faster than the speed of light. That restriction ensures that teleported information obeys the cosmic speed limit.
>
> Even though teleportation does not allow superluminal communication, it does provide a detour around another physics blockade known as the *no-cloning theorem*. That theorem states that one cannot perfectly copy a quantum object to, for instance, send a facsimile to another person. But teleportation does not create a copy per se—it simply shifts the quantum information from one place to another, destroying the original in the process.*

---

* Matson, John (2012). Quantum Teleportation Achieved over Record Distances. *Nature*, 13 August 2012. http://www.nature.com/news/quantum-teleportation-achieved-over-record-distances-1.11163

The paradox has vanished and the mystery of entanglement is solved by considering entangled photons as a whole system. States are not physical objects subject to the limits of energy and mass. They are not conjugate pairs. Quantum cryptography obeys the Heisenberg Uncertainty Principle, operates within the speed limit of light, and satisfies Einstein's sense of realism. At the time this was written, several for-profit companies were in the early stages of building quantum key distribution networks operating over long distances through fiber optical transmission lines.

WHEN CAN I GET ONE?

It is interesting to reflect on the struggle of the early pioneers of quantum mechanics to get it right. Even Einstein had difficulty separating classical physics thinking from quantum physics thinking. His references to realism and predeterminism reveal a lingering connection with deep philosophical ideas that held back European science for centuries. Europeans, for example, rejected the idea of zero and infinity until the 1400s. Newton did not appear on the scene until the 1600s. Einstein's relativity theory was not immediately accepted following his 1905 paper. Classical thought was still part of the DNA of modern physics even in the 1930s. Systems thinking, as it is now called, was unknown by most people even in the 1950s. Quantum theory must have been a difficult pill to swallow.

Action at a distance through quantum superposition is easy to reject even in the twenty-first century, because it rubs our intuition the wrong way. But then, so do most of probability theory and the quantification of chance. Ask anyone delving in the stock market if they truly believe in *regression to the mean*, and they will probably shrug it off when the market soars and blame market corrections on some economic or political factor when it goes down.

The sophons of Trisolaran is science fiction, but quantum cryptography is not. It is real. Starting from the EPR paradox thought experiment that Einstein thought rendered entanglement as science fiction, entanglement has been repeatedly demonstrated to work on Earth and in space. It is only a matter of time before quantum cryptography jumps from the lab to commercial products that make the signal far more secure than current technology allows.

Recent experiments on prime number cracking suggest that the Diffie–Hellman–Merkle concept and RSA algorithm are doomed. Eventually, quantum computers using Shor's algorithm will be able to factor large numbers into their prime factors faster than the Internet will be able to replace them. But, quantum computing can also provide a workaround using quantum cryptography. By the time you read this, Quantum Key Distribution (QKD) may already be routine.

In 2016, Devin Power writing in *Popular Science* magazine said,

> QKD systems are becoming a reality. The first quantum transaction took place in 2004, when researchers in Vienna used entangled photons to transfer a 3,000-Euro deposit into their bank account. Commercial QKD systems came to the United States in 2013, when R&D nonprofit Battelle installed a fiber optic network protected by encrypted photons. The system, developed by ID Quantique, had already used its technology to protect the results of an election in Geneva in 2007.*

The signal will continue to be correct and secure for a long time into the future. But, the Internet will never be the same.

---

* Powell, Devin (2016). What Is Quantum Cryptography? *Popular Science*, Mar 3, 2016. https://www.popsci.com/what-is-quantum-cryptography

Signals from Hell

IN THE SUMMER OF 1976, IBM invited my colleagues and me to teach a short course on computer science topics to career IBM'ers working out of San Jose, California and the Almaden Research Labs, where relational databases were invented. The gig was partly a reward and partly educational for seasoned employees of the dominant computer company. So management rented classroom space at the University of California's newest campus located on top of a mountain outside of Santa Cruz. The view of the Pacific Ocean was magnificent, and the participants challenging.

Civilization bumps up against High Street on the west side and a bucolic open field pans out on the east side of Highway 1 that runs north and south along the Central Coast of California near Santa Cruz. Turning right at Bay Street my car begins a 1,000-foot climb up the side of the mountain where classrooms, dorms, and offices are perched. The road circles the Great Meadow and soon brings me to a cluster of dorms and classrooms where the instruction is to take place. UC Santa Cruz is in the middle of a redwood forest overlooking the Pacific Ocean mostly hidden by rolling fog. But, today was different—I could almost reach out and touch the blue sea.

Professor Huffman founded the Computer Science Department and led it for many years. Drawn by its beauty and proximity to surfing in the Jack O'Neill way, Huffman occasionally joined us at lunch in one of the cafeterias.* On one occasion he told the story of the institution, and its attempts to liberalize higher education. The school was heavily influenced

---

* O'Neill invented the wetsuit. https://duckduckgo.com/?q=Jack+O'Reilley%2C+surfer&t=h_&ia=about

by the counter-culture shaping up in nearby San Francisco, and promoted an unusual openness. For example, professors gave written evaluations rather than grades.

The "no grading" experiment eventually faded, and so did another experiment. Initially students configured their own housing. The university provided large empty spaces and an invitation to students to build their own environments. Bathrooms were co-educational, and kitchens were communal. Over time, this freewheeling environment began to self-organize into "private property" and borders. A kind of "us" versus "them" developed. Apparently, students were more comfortable with their own tribe, living a structured life with strict rules of behavior and established social norms rather than the freewheeling lifestyle of the counter culture. While each tribe had different norms, the unstructured society gave way to structure. Belonging to a tribe was more important than flaunting one's individualism.

Forty years later, the same self-organizing behavior is evident in the largest community on Earth—Facebook.com. At the time of this writing, Facebook.com had over 2 billion subscribers with approximately 185 million active on a daily basis. But most of them formed tribes with fewer than a few hundred, or perhaps thousand members. Facebook.com users wall themselves off much like the students at UC Santa Cruz did in the 1970s.

Self-organization is a type of network effect where nodes (nodes are users or actors) with many followers attract even more followers. This feedback effect ends up creating hubs, or extremely connected actors. The topology of the social network begins to look like a collection of "us" versus "them" tribes. The topology of self-organization is shown in Figure 10.1 as hubs with tribal members following a handful of leaders. Rather than a freewheeling "random network," the social network is lumpy with a few highly connected leaders and a multitude of barely connected followers. It is a herd-like structure.

The Internet provides the ability to connect anyone to nearly everyone else on the planet, and yet most social network consumers prefer to connect with people that think and act like them. This is called *homophily*, literally meaning, "love of self." An article in *The New York Times Magazine* explains homophily very clearly,

In the 1950s, sociologists coined the term "homophily"—love of the same—to explain our inexorable tendency to link up with one another in ways that confirm rather than test our core beliefs. Those who liked Ike, in other words, liked each other. The term didn't catch on, but the concept is now enjoying a renaissance, in part because it has been repeatedly invoked to explain the American electorate's apparent polarization into equally self-regarding camps.

"Similarity breeds connection," the sociologists Miller McPherson, Lynn Smith-Lovin, and James Cook wrote in their classic 2001 paper on the subject, "Birds of a Feather: Homophily in Social Networks," and "the result is that people's personal networks are homogeneous." This year, other academics have cited homophily in elucidating everything from why teenagers choose friends who smoke and drink the same amount that they do to "the strong isolation of lower-class blacks from the interracial-marriage market." Researchers at MIT even published "Homophily in Online Dating: When Do You Like Someone Like Yourself?" which showed that you like someone like yourself most of the time, online or off. So much for "opposites attract."*

FIGURE 10.1 This Facebook.com network contains 4,039 nodes and 16,384 links, arranged as a collection of hub-and-spoke communities. Data provided by http://snap.stanford.edu.

---

* Retica, Aaron (2006). Homophily. *The New York Times Magazine*, Dec. 10, 2006. https://www.nytimes.com/2006/12/10/magazine/10Section2a.t-4.html

The signal is no longer a simple mathematical equation for transmitting information. It depends on who creates it, and how it spreads. It has become the voice of the online herd. Homophily drowns out the individual and replaces it with a single carrier wave—the *social meme*. A social meme is a virally transmitted symbol or idea created from the combustive interaction of online tribes. Derived from the concept of a *selfish meme* as defined and studied by Clinton Richard Dawkins (1941–)—an English evolutionary biologist—the social meme has become the signal.* It has replaced individual thought with groupthink in much of online discourse.

In the 1970s, television was the message as well as the medium. In the 2000s, the Internet is the message as well as the medium. The Internet signal carries more than information—it carries meaning in the form of a social meme. That is, content is part information bits and part subtle association—who sends the signal and when it is received are as important as the information bits. This often works in favor of humanity, but sometimes it backfires. In the twenty-first century, we have created a global platform for spreading both good and bad memes.

Sometimes the social meme is a signal from hell.

CHIRPING IN CONSPIRACY NETWORKS

Concerns about the spread of fake news memes, and online persuasion have stimulated deeper study of influence in highly connected online networks such as Facebook.com and Twitter.com. Not only do humans influence one another through repetition or reputation-oriented influence, but machines and the technology to aggregate and rapidly spread memes throughout a tribe exercises great influence over humans. The spread of social memes can result in actions. Even more disturbing is the fact that online actors need not be human. Much of what humans consume is machine generated by bots. A 2017 study of the 2016 US presidential elections by Oxford University reported, "that bots reached positions of measurable influence during the 2016 US election."† Machines posing as human actors influenced voters. The machine has become the message as much as people using the Internet to spread memes. In the twenty-first century, facts matter less than how memes are spread and promoted. Repetition, groupthink, herd mentality, and passion trump reason.

---

* Dawkins, C. R. (1976). *The Selfish Gene*. Oxford University Press. ISBN 0-19-286092-5.

† Wooley, S.C. and D. R. Guilbeault. (2017). Computational Propaganda in the United State of America: Manufacturing Consensus Online. http://comprop.oii.ox.ac.uk/wp-content/uploads/sites/89/2017/06/Comprop-USA.pdf

Bots have become indistinguishable from humans and therefore meme-spreading bots have become as believable as meme-spreading humans. The medium counts as much as the message.

The signal is both content and transmission, but transmission appears to have the persuasive upper hand. Connectivity is the main driver. Social connections are links that transmit memes from actor to actor (bot-to-bot, bot-to-human, as well as human-to-human) through their online postings. Posting a meme that spreads to other actors is called *chirping*, here, and networks that create an avalanche of *agreement* are called *conspiracy networks*. By agreement we mean that all or nearly all of the actors agree with or support the posted meme. Agreement is assigned a value in [0, 1], such that 1 represents complete agreement, 0 represents complete disagreement, and actor state $0 < s < 1$ represents partial agreement. A conspiracy forms when a majority of actors agree with $s > 1/2$ regardless of the facts.

Intuitively, social networks act as amplifiers of both truth and false information in such a convincing manner that it is sometimes difficult to distinguish one from the other. It is generally accepted that greater connectivity of actors increases the impact of information as it spreads from actor to actor. Network connectivity matters, but the exact nature of how topology impacts influence across entire networks has not been fully explored. Less is known about the dynamics of meme spreading outside of epidemic models that treat it as a form of contagion.

Attempts to control the flow of information through a social network by censorship or blocking are unlikely to succeed for a number of reasons: determining what is true and what is fake may be difficult; identification and response to outbreaks of viral information may be economically impossible in a timely manner due to the size of the network and speed of spreading; and censuring may be considered bad for business. Determining the appropriateness of an online posting is also a subjective decision process that is highly cultural and personal. Such a determination may not be possible due to varying tastes among consumers.

An alternative approach to control meme spreading is to exercise a form of self-organization that "steers" the flow of information through a network by relying on topological controls. We know, for example, that in an epidemic network, actors with high connectivity exercise more control (spreading) overall, than actors with low connectivity. We also know that high betweenness actors—middlemen and middlewomen—may act as blocking nodes when their removal separates the network into islands.

These subtle forms of control are more likely to be accepted by consumers than an authoritarian controller. The approach described here is based on the simple idea of "fighting fire with fire," or more precisely, "fighting fire by starting a backfire." This may be implemented through human or automated means, e.g., using bots to control other humans and bots.

The central question is, "Does topology matter and if so, is it possible to control or steer the spread of information through a social network by exploiting network topology?" I claim that *the spread of influence of memes can be controlled and dampened by counter measures whose sum of influence is equal to or greater than the influence of an opposing meme.* This requires a definition of influence that is compatible with how memes spread. In turn, the definition of influence depends on an analytical model of spreading.

Generally, a viral meme spreads through a network by adjacency, i.e., actors influence adjacent actors. A meme might die out or spread without attenuation until it eventually reaches all connected actors. The meme may become weakened as it spreads, leaving actors in a partial state $0 < s < 1$. It is possible that a viral meme oscillates between poles of a bi-stable system representing the oscillations of undecided actors. Therefore, we must decide if the network is stable and if it is, how a counter measure can steer the network into a desirable and stable end state.

The strategy of a meme promoter is to spread a post throughout the entire network in a convincing manner so that the state of every actor is $s = 1.0$ (conspirator). The strategy of a contrarian is the opposite: to convince all actors to adopt the contrary state $s = 0$ (contrary). Generally, actors in a state $s < 1/2$ are contrarians, and actors in a state $s > 1/2$ are conspirators. Conspirators and contrarians compete to drive online actors toward $s = 1$ or $s = 0$. Realistically, competition among conspirators and contrarians drives actors to some partial state $0 < s < 1$.

The final state of a stable peer-pressure social network can be controlled by assigning $s = 0$ to a small number of actors. This is possible when the sum of influences of the contrary actors exceeds the sum of influences of conspirator's actors and the network synchronizes. The contrarian actor's states are pinned at $s = 0$, and the conspirator actor's states are pinned at $s = 1$. All other actors lie somewhere in-between.

Assume the network is a closed system such that only other actors in the network influence an actor. Because influence is communicated by adjacency, state s_i of actor n_i changes only because of its adjacent neighbors. Memes flow through the network by "contaminating" nearest neighbors.

The flow of a meme from actor to actor may be amplified or attenuated by repetition. It may oscillate between upper and lower values due to social pressure from peers. It may eventually die out. Stability depends on the network's topology.

CHIRPING NETWORKS

Watts* describes the behavior of a certain species of cricket found in South America to illustrate how a random network synchronizes and becomes an orderly network simply because of nearest-neighbor connections. Crickets listen, chirp, listen, chirp, etc. at random, initially. Over time, they all listen at the same time and chirp at the same time. That is, they synchronize without any central authority or external control mechanism. Lewis[†] showed that the transition from chaotic chirping to orchestrated chirping is inevitable in some networks and not in others, depending on the topology of the interconnections.

Networks that repeatedly cycle through states in lock-step fashion are said to oscillate, and networks containing nodes that reach a common value are said to stabilize. A third possibility exists—networks that are so unstable that the states of some or all of its nodes "blow up" or rapidly increase/decrease without bound. Such erratic networks are inherently unstable. Regardless of the eventual state of a network, the states of its nodes may behave erratically over a short period of time before stabilizing. We call such behavior *chaotic*, when states change erratically and unpredictably.

A dynamic network is said to *sync* if, starting at some initial state, $S(0)$, it evolves in finite time to another state, $S(t^*)$, and stays there, forever. We call $S(t^*)$ a *strange attractor*, and if the network remains at its strange attractor point indefinitely, it is also a *fixed point*. Networks that appear to bounce around from one state to another in no apparent pattern are considered *chaotic*. Networks that oscillate between two or more strange attractors are called *oscillators*. Oscillators are also considered to be *pseudo-stable*. Pseudo-stable nodes often oscillate much like a bi-stable oscillator, or *flip-flop* device in a computer, so we also call them *bi-stable* nodes and networks.

State transitions from $s_i(0)$, to $s_i(1)$, $s_i(2)$ ... $s_i(t^*)$ form a *trajectory* in state space defined by plotting $s_i(t+1)$ along the vertical axis, and $s_i(t)$

---

* Watts, Duncan (2004). *Six Degrees: The Science of a Connected Age.* Norton.
† Lewis, Ted G. (2006). *Network Science: Theory and Applications.* John Wiley & Sons.

along the horizontal axis of a chaotic map. A *chaotic map* is simply a plot of a node's trajectory in state space. Figure 10.2 illustrates the map of a stable node, bi-stable node, and chaotic node. A *stable node* is attracted to its fixed point regardless of its starting point. The bi-stable node oscillates between two or more points, and the chaotic node traces out an apparently erratic walk. More generally, the trajectory of a chaotic node traces out the same erratic path, over and over again. It is not truly random, but rather, non-linear.

What follows shows that under certain conditions, chaotic, bi-stable, and stable states can be induced in social networks by either *pinning* or *re-wiring* connections. The purpose, of course, is to steer the network toward a desirable stable state. Pinning is the process of inserting a beacon actor

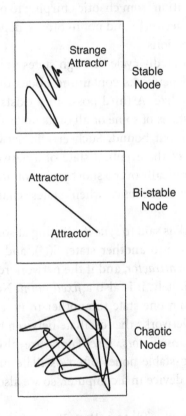

FIGURE 10.2 Possible trajectories of a node in a network include stable, bi-stable, and chaotic. Stable trajectories reach a fixed point; bi-stable trajectories oscillate between or among multiple points or poles; and chaotic trajectories follow no apparent pattern.

with periodic signaling to ultimately synchronize the entire network.* Re-wiring is more subtle than pinning. Its goal is to alter the topology of the network such that its trajectory automatically reaches a desirable fixed point. We examine mechanisms for achieving sync in simple chirping networks, and peer-pressure networks that evolve the state of every actor toward the average of neighboring states.

Networks that synchronize, reaching a consensus across actors, are considered conspiracies in the most general sense of the word. A conspiracy starts with a single post by one actor and spreads throughout the network, driving it to a certain fixed point. A non-conspiratorial network, on the other hand, dissipates a single post so that it has little impact on the state of the network, or causes it to oscillate and never reach a consensus. The author sidesteps the question of whether conspiracies are "good" or "bad," and focuses on how to manage them. For simplicity, conspirators are actors pinned at state $s = 1$ that seek to convince other actors to also adopt a state of $s = 1$. Contrarians are pinned at $s = 0$ and seek to drive the states of other actors to $s = 0$, also. Typically, all other actors seek a fixed point somewhere in between, $0 < s < 1$. This assignment is arbitrary and can be reversed without loss of generality.

Chirping crickets sync whenever an actor is pinned, but any network syncs whenever the topology of the network is aperiodic. A network is aperiodic if it contains cycles of lengths that are relatively prime to one another. Since every number is relatively prime to 3, a social network with a cycle of length 3 is sufficient to cause it to sync. Social networks such as Facebook are notoriously clustered with many cycles of length 3, so it can be assumed they sync. A bigger question is, "What fixed point will a synchronizing social network reach if one or more of its actors are pinned?"

PEER-PRESSURE NETWORKS

Atay, Bikikoglu, and Jost[†] studied a general type of synchronizing network where the next state of node i is determined by the difference between its current state and the average state of adjacent nodes. That is, each actor is subject to *peer pressure* and tends to fall in line with its neighbors. The state of an *Atay network* node increases in value if the average difference across

---

* Wang, X. and G. Chen (2002). Pinning Control of Scale-Free Dynamical Networks. *Physica A*, 310, pp. 521–531.

† Atay, F. M., T. Biyikoglu, and J. Jost (2006). Synchronization of Networks with Prescribed Degree Distributions. *IEEE Transaction on Cycles and Systems I*, 53(1), pp. 92–98.

nearest neighbors is greater than the node's current state, and decreases by
the average difference if less than its current value:

$$s_i(t+1) = s_i(t) + \sum_j \frac{s_j(t) - s_i(t)}{d_i}$$

Under what condition does the state equation lead to synchronization
when applied to social network S? If the Atay network synchronizes, all
actors reach a consensus, possibly forming a conspiracy network. If it
oscillates, no consensus is reached, and therefore, no conspiracy is formed.
Finally, a conspiracy is reached if a value of 1.0 in one node spreads to all
other nodes such that they synchronize with a value of $s \geq 1/2$. The degree
of conspiracy formation is represented by the average value of actor's states
across all actors, if and when the network syncs. By agreement, a conspiracy forms when the average fixed point is $s \geq 1/2$ across all other actors.

Figure 10.3 shows the trajectories of two Atay networks: 1) one is stable
and eventually achieves a stable fixed point, and the other 2) is bi-stable
and oscillates between two strange attractors. In most cases, Atay networks
either synchronize by reaching a strange attractor or oscillate between bi-
stable values, forever. Because the degree term, d_i, acts as a dampening
factor, an Atay network never "blows up." But, what determines whether
an Atay network achieves a transient bi-stable state or reaches a state of
synchronization? Furthermore, how can the final state be managed?

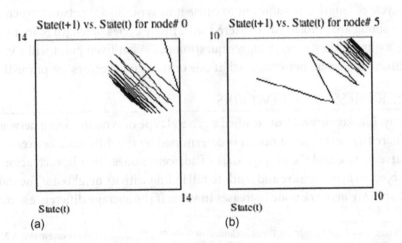

FIGURE 10.3 Chaotic map of Atay network trajectories: (a) node that reaches
its strange attractor as the network syncs, and (b) node that oscillates about two
attractors as the network does not sync.

COUNTER MEASURES

The model just described suggests means of controlling the state of a social network by pinning contrarian actors at strategic locations in the network, e.g., at high-influence nodes. Assuming the actor with the most influence is pinned at $s = 1$. This represents the worst-case scenario of unrestricted meme spreading. Regardless of the initial states of other actors, the peer-pressure network syncs with $s = 1$, forming a conspiracy network.

Suppose we select k other actors at random such that the sum of their influences exceeds the pinned conspirator's influence. The peer-pressure network synchronizes with an average value less than 1/2. Table 10.1 summarizes this result for the chirping network, a scale-free network with 500 nodes and 2,000 links, a random network with 500 nodes and 2,000 links, and two Facebook.com sub-networks provided by SNAP.* A network is scale-free if it has a large central hub. A network is random if nodes are connected to one another by randomly selecting node pairs.

In each case, the actor with the most influence is designated a conspirator and pinned at $s = 1.0$. But a conspiracy does not form if the sum of influences of k other actors exceeds the influence of the conspiracy actor. The number of contrarians, k, is determined simply by selecting nodes at random and summing their influence until it exceeds the influence of the conspirator. This number is expressed as a percentage of nodes in Table 10.1.

A simple cricket Chirp network syncs with average actor state at $s = 0.39$ when 25% of its seven nodes are pinned at $s = 0$. The Facebook network of 713 actors syncs with average actor state of $s = 0.47$ when 4.0% of its nodes are pinned at $s = 0$. In general, the larger a network, the smaller fraction of contrarians are needed to block the conspiracy. The Facebook 713 network contains 713 nodes, 2,000 links, and two central hubs of degree 360

TABLE 10.1   Summary of Results for Counter Measures

Network	% Contrary Nodes	Fixed Point
Chirp	25.0%	0.39
Scale-free 500	4.2%	0.4
Random 500	0.7%	0.42
Facebook 713	4.0%	0.47
Facebook 4039	1.1%	0.39

---

* http://snap.stanford.edu

and 347 connections, respectively. The Facebook 4,039 network contains 4,039 nodes and 16,384 links. Only 1.1% or an average of 45.4 contrarians are needed to prevent a conspiracy initiated by the most influential node (which is the secondary hub with 347 connections). As the size of the network grows, the number of contrarians required to halt the spread of influence emanating from a conspirator declines as a percentage of nodes.

Contrarian actor effectiveness declines according to a power law, see Figure 10.4. If no contrarian is pinned at $s = 0$, the network synchronizes at $s = 1$. As the number of randomly chosen contrarians increases, the average value of actor states declines as $O(1/k)$. For Facebook 713, the average state drops below 0.5 when 28.5 actors (4.0%) are pinned at $s = 0$. There is a diminishing return on contrarian meme spreading.

Conclusion: pinning a relatively small percentage of contrarian actors can control meme spreading in peer-pressure networks. The state of the social network can be controlled to any desired level by increasing the percentage of pinned contrarians. However, the effectiveness of contrarians declines inversely with number of pinned contrarians.

No attempt was made to optimize the results presented here by selecting contrarians. The pinned conspirator is always the highest influence node and the contrarians are chosen at random. Selecting the conspirator at random and choosing the contrarians with the largest influence produces much stronger results. The key to understanding the behavior of social networks lies in the sum of influences of conspirators and contrarians. It is how power is defined in the network.

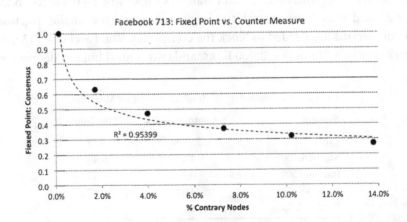

FIGURE 10.4 Effectiveness of contrarian pinning declines according to a power law. Each point was obtained by averaging over ten simulated conspiracies.

APPROXIMATING INFLUENCE

What is influence? Mathematically, influence is like gravity—the gravitational pull is greater when a body (node) is nearby than when it is far away. However, gravitational pull acts on a body (node) even if it is separated from other bodies by large distances. Influence in a social network is similar: nearest neighbors exert immediate influence while neighbors of neighbors exert less influence, and neighbors of neighbors of neighbors exert even less influence.

Influence is computed by *repeated* averaging of values stored in adjacent nodes. Initially, the value at each node is set to its degree, which is equal to the number of connecting links attached to each node. This value is replaced by the average of nearest-neighbor node values and then normalized by dividing by the largest value over all nodes. As averaging repeats, less influential nodes decrease in value faster than more influential nodes. Eventually, values stabilize at a number representing the node's influence relative to other node's influence. Typically, convergence occurs after fewer than 100 iterations. The final numerical value of influence is obtained by multiplying all values by the largest value obtained after convergence. This normalization typically produces a number greater than 1.0, representing the "leverage" a node has over its nearest neighbors and neighbors of neighbors.

COMMENT

Signaling within a social network has crossed a border separating information content, i.e., facts, from persuasion, i.e., memes devoid of factual content. In some ways, social meme spreading takes humanity backward in time when tribal leaders and custom dictated what we chose to believe. It ranks with the all-time notorious belief that the universe revolves around the Earth or that diseases are acts of God. It throws us back to the time when most people believed what they were told to believe by a higher authority. It is belief without proof—an anti-intellectual throwback to pre-scientific revolution times.

More formally, most self-organizing networks tend to evolve from high entropy to low entropy. That is, unstructured and somewhat random networks change over time and become more structured, more centralized, and more dogmatic. This is the underlying mechanism of preferential attachment studied by network scientists. It occurs so often in nature and human endeavors that preferential attachment is almost a law of nature.

In any complex system such as Facebook.com or Twitter.com, self-organization and the decline of entropy can be reversed only by exerting effort to reverse the flow of entropy. It takes energy to move a system from low-to-high entropy. For example, deconstructing a network as illustrated in Figure 10.1 requires an injection of randomness. Instead of clusters around a large hub, a random network has little or no structure, hence its name.

To offset preferential attachment, someone or something must re-wire the connections among nodes such the number of connections of highly connected hubs are reduced and the number of connections of marginally connected nodes are increased. This is equivalent to a form of democratization that gives every actor a voice and dissipates the power of hubs. Such societies are more likely to survive disruption. Such social networks are more likely to be sustainable over long periods of time.

An overly powerful influence in a social network can be offset by re-wiring connections to increase entropy and pin contrarians such that the sum of their influences exceeds the influence of any one actor.

Index

Printed in the United States
by Baker & Taylor Publisher Services